Shawn Johnson

Gymnastics' Golden Girl

GymnStars
VOLUME 1

CREATIVE MEDIA, INC.
PO Box 6270
Whittier, California 90609-6270
United States of America

WWW.CREATIVEMEDIA.NET

Front cover photo by Jasmin Schneebeli-Wochner
Back cover photos by Ricardo Bufolin
Cover and Book design by Joseph Dzidrums

First Edition: January 2012

Library of Congress Control Number: 2012930354

ISBN 978-0-9835393-2-2   10 9 8 7 6 5 4 3 2 1

Shawn Johnson

Gymnastics' Golden Girl

GymnStars
VOLUME 1

A Biography by
Christine Dzidrums
and
Leah Rendon

Special thanks to:

Elizabeth Allison
Ricardo Bufolin
Joseph Dzidrums
Gene5535
Jamie Lantzy
Jerry Logsdon
Don McLaughlin
Scott Fuller
Jasmin Schneebeli-Wochner
Tomas Tyrpekl

Love to:
Joshua and Timothy

Contents

"In my eyes, I've never failed because I've never given anything less than my best."

A Rocky Beginning

Serene, powdery snow lined the streets of a Midwest American town. Doug and Teri Johnson drove anxiously, but cautiously, through Des Moines, Iowa's snowplowed streets.

Doug and Teri met as teenagers while kicking up their heels at a local roller skating rink. The young couple soon fell in love. Teri, a pretty blonde cheerleader, possessed a bubbly personality and a bright smile. A varsity football and baseball player, Doug sported shaggy hair, kind eyes and a friendly face.

After high school graduation, the couple married and began their respective careers. Doug worked as a contractor, while Teri secured a job at an insurance company.

As Doug drove onto Pleasant Street, Teri glanced anxiously at the 88-bed brick hospital that awaited them. Any moment now, they would welcome their first child into their lives.

Several hours later, their daughter, Shawn Machel Johnson, entered the world, but the pale infant's chance of survival looked grim. The umbilical cord had wrapped around her neck. Doctors could not locate her pulse or heartbeat. In addition, her reflexes and muscle tone were also absent.

In the first minute of a baby's life, he or she undergoes a standard test called the APGAR. During this brief exam, a medical professional checks the infant's physical condition and assigns it a health score from 0-10 with 10 being highest. Shawn scored a devastating 0.

Teri and Doug, who had waited fifteen years for a child, held their breath as the medical staff attended to their baby girl. Suddenly, Baby Shawn began displaying what would become one of her trademark features – an indomitable toughness. Her heart began beating again. The newborn's breathing grew stronger. She even wiggled when a doctor applied tiny pressure to her body. Before long, her skin turned a healthy pink from her head to her tiny toes.

Shawn's parents exhaled in relief and hugged one another tightly. Their daughter would be just fine. She had passed her first major challenge in life.

Doctors later told the Johnsons that Shawn almost hadn't lived, but the tough baby girl prevailed after all. From that moment on, the couple referred to their precious daughter as their miracle baby.

Many hours later, nurses handed Baby Shawn to her proud new parents. Teri looked at her beloved daughter wrapped up in a fluffy, warm blanket with a delicate pink cap on her head.

"Look," an emotional Doug exclaimed, motioning to his baby. "She's smiling!"

Iowa, Heartland of America
(Photo by Joseph Dzidrums)

"I'm a daredevil with a big smile."

Lively Toddler

An energetic toddler bursting with energy, Shawn flurried about the house so much, her parents could barely keep up with her! In fact, they sometimes placed their daughter in her playpen just so they could catch their breath. But Shawn quickly learned to climb up the sides of the small enclosure. Before long, she even began using the baby furniture to perform pull-ups!

Most babies turn into crawlers by the latter half of their first year. Not peppy Shawn. She skipped the crawling stage entirely! One day her parents sat chatting when seven-month-old Shawn walked casually into the room! Teri and Doug looked at her in shock and disbelief! Their little girl had crawled out of her crib!

Shawn mostly loved to jump. She often piled her toys into a giant mountain and scaled to its top. From there, she would climb onto the family's entertainment center and dive onto a red leather couch nearby.

Shawn's parents also noticed that their little girl loved music and danced enthusiastically to it whenever she heard it. They felt inspired to enroll their toddler in a dance class. Truth be told, they also hoped that the lessons would curb her extra energy.

Shawn liked dance classes – for a while. Then she grew inattentive in class. So Shawn's parents registered her in a tumbling class. Except that activity eventually bored her, too.

Teri and Doug wondered how they might ever tame their daughter's energy. Would she ever find a structured activity that sustained her interest?

As the months passed, Shawn's adventurous spirit knew no limits. One afternoon the little girl ran aimlessly throughout the house when she stumbled and bumped her head. When the toddler began bleeding, a panicked Teri and Doug raced her to the hospital. A doctor performed several stitches on her head just to close her wound!

The scary incident didn't alter Shawn's rambunctiousness, though. One day Teri entered the family kitchen and discovered the young girl standing on the dinner table! Before she could order her daughter down, Shawn hurled herself into her father's arms.

Of course! Why hadn't she thought of it sooner? Gymnastics! The difficult, highly physical sport would challenge her smart daughter and utilize her overflowing energy. In fact, gymnastics presented so many apparatuses that Shawn might never tire of it.

Teri's favorite part about gymnastics? Soft floor mats would surround Shawn at all times, allowing her active daughter to climb, run and jump endlessly. If she took an unexpected spill, soft foam would protect her!

On Shawn's first day at gymnastics class, her eyes darted to the balance beam. The trademark apparatus in women's gymnastics, the long, raised beam with legs on each end usually measures about four inches wide. In a typical balance beam routine, the gymnast performs many skills: connecting dance elements, turns, acrobatic tricks and a dismount. Many gymnastics experts consider it the sport's toughest piece of equipment. Naturally, the balance beam intrigued Shawn the most.

Vault, floor and uneven bars round out women's gymnastics' other events. Shawn's shiny, bright eyes also looked toward those apparatuses with great interest. She felt very excited and curious about gymnastics.

Not surprisingly, Shawn's incredible energy extended into gym class. She didn't like the listening part of gymnastics. When an instructor would sit students on mats and explain a new exercise, Shawn would jump up and run to the balance beam. Then the teacher became cross with her for interrupting class.

While the students waited patiently in a single file line to work on an apparatus, Shawn bounced restlessly as she awaited her chance. When her turn ended, she would dash to the front of the line again, anxious to try a new trick.

Shawn also loved learning gymnastics' basics. She mastered somersaults, cartwheels and even handsprings. In fact, the bubbly girl quickly surpassed the other beginning gymnasts in her group.

Meanwhile, back at the Johnson home, Shawn's parents welcomed their active daughter into nearly every aspect of their lives. Whenever Teri vacuumed the home, her rambunctious toddler often climbed aboard the device and rode it as Mom moved from room to room. On one occasion, while still wearing diapers, Shawn even helped her father paint the house!

When Teri and Doug completed daily tasks, they often played with their little girl. Shawn owned a toy pink convertible that she adored. When weather permitted, her parents would watch carefully as she sat in the driver's seat of her beloved car and zoomed around the driveway.

Although an only child, Shawn never longed for company. When her parents were busy, she played with her dog, Dude, a Long-Haired Golden Retriever, who had entered the Johnson family long before Shawn was born. The little girl loved Dude and considered him her best friend.

Shawn also claimed a large extended family. She adored her aunts, uncles and cousins dearly. One of her favorite outings? When the entire family met at a restaurant for a special dinner. Shawn loved laughing with her family as they shared funny stories.

In particular, Shawn felt close to her slightly older cousin, Tori. Both girls, with golden blonde hair and bright smiles, could easily pass as sisters. That's exactly how Shawn and Tori viewed one another, too. They were often inseparable.

Wherever the Johnsons went, people always commented on Shawn's happy nature. The young girl rarely stopped smiling. Little did she know that one day the world would fall in love with her contagious smile!

As Shawn's obvious talent for gymnastics grew, so did her impatience. She picked up skills faster than children twice her age. The budding gymnast constantly craved more apparatus time and additional personal instruction.

One day Teri flipped through the local newspaper when an advertisement caught her eye. Just down the street, a new gym celebrated its grand opening. As a new business, the classes were still small. That meant Shawn would receive crucial one-on-one time with an experienced coach. That settled it. She would switch Shawn to this new gym.

Little did Teri realize that her idea would not only affect her family's lives, it would alter the world of elite gymnastics forever.

Shawn's Million Dollar Smile
(Photo by Jamie Lantzy)

On Chow: "He's everything - he's my coach, my second parent, my friend,"

Liang Chow

A key member of the Chinese Men's Gymnastics National Team, Liang Chow forged a long, successful career. He won more than 30 international medals, including a bronze medal at the 1989 World Championships and gold at the Asian Games.

Gymnastics smiled on Chow's personal life, too. Through his beloved sport, he met his girlfriend, Liwen Zhuang, a fellow gymnast. The dainty athlete competed for many years as part of China's national team.

In the early 1990s, Chow officially retired from gymnastics. He then began planning a move to the United States. When the University of Iowa, located in America's heartland, offered him an English scholarship, he eagerly accepted.

Like most newcomers in an unfamiliar setting, Chow felt shell-shocked when he arrived in the U.S. Because China treats their gymnasts like celebrities, even completing daily tasks for them, he needed to learn how to cook meals, clean his apartment and wash his laundry all on his own.

Chow also strengthened his English skills. He brushed up on his new language by watching American television. In particular, he enjoyed tuning in to David Letterman's talk show.

Liang Chow, Shawn's Coach
(Photo by Ricardo Bufolin)

For the first time in his life, Chow supported himself financially. He began assisting the University of Iowa's men's and women's gymnastics teams. The former gymnast enjoyed passing down his knowledge to a younger generation.

Chow returned to China once and proposed to Liwen. The young couple married in a modest ceremony. Then Liwen accompanied her new husband back to the United States. Several years later they welcomed a son, Kevin, into their lives.

After Chow earned his college degree, he set his sights on opening his own training gym. After careful consideration, he and his family moved 116 miles west to Iowa's state capital, Des Moines, and opened Chow's Gymnastics and Dance Institute.

Chow loved running his own gym. He believed that every child should be trained in a loving and positive environment. The kind man always smiled and never raised his voice. When a child misbehaved, he merely frowned at them until they straightened out their act.

In his gym's mission statement, Chow described his institute as a first-class training center in a loving and supportive atmosphere. He stressed that his gym provided important lessons to children. They would learn confidence, self-esteem, self-discipline and responsibility.

One fateful day, a six-year-old and her mother marched into his gym. The young girl's tiny size belied her huge desire. She hoped to become a great gymnast and would work hard to achieve that goal.

"From day one we realized this kid was really special, because she loves learning and wants to reach her potential," Chow later told *Sports Illustrated.*

"My name is Coach Chow," the gym owner told the little girl. "It's nice to meet you."

The young gymnast looked up at the slight man. He had a friendly face and a kind demeanor. She liked him instantly.

"I'm Shawn," she smiled.

Coach Chow suppressed a grin. The budding gymnast's goofy smile revealed many missing baby teeth.

"What's your favorite event?" Chow asked her.

"The balance beam," Shawn responded without hesitation.

During her first lesson that afternoon, Shawn fidgeted while awaiting her turn on the balance beam. Finally, she grew restless, darted out of line and performed a perfect cartwheel on a nearby floor mat. Then she returned to her spot in line for the beam.

Teri held her breath while she watched the scene unfold. Her daughter's former coaches often became irritated with the young girl's impatience. Chow, on the other hand, merely laughed with delight at Shawn's enthusiasm.

"I love her energy," he smiled good-naturedly.

Teri immediately relaxed. She had a great feeling about Shawn's new coach and felt instantly grateful that she had brought her daughter to this specific gym.

Coach and student immediately clicked. Chow challenged Shawn, and she worked hard to please him. After just a week at his gym, the eager whiz kid acquired a back handspring!

Before long, Shawn owned tricks and routines more difficult than girls twice her age! Sensing he might have a future champion on his hands, Chow asked Doug and Teri for permission to move their six-year old daughter to the pre-teen advanced group, where the girls competed against other gyms.

Shawn's parents felt very reluctant to place their daughter in competitive gymnastics. They wanted the sport to remain a fun activity for Shawn. Would she still enjoy gymnastics if she began competing?

"Why can't she remain with girls her own age?" they asked Chow.

The Johnsons' response floored Chow. Having spent his entire life in gymnastics, he encountered many overly ambitious parents who pushed their child into the sport, even when he or she showed little interest in it. Now he had a student who loved the sport and possessed genuine talent for it, but her parents weren't interested in grooming her for stardom. Chow found their laidback attitude surprisingly refreshing.

Shawn's parents later discussed the possibility with their daughter. Her eyes instantly lit up at the idea of training in a

Iowa City - Chow's First American Home
(Photo by Joseph Dzidrums)

higher group and participating in competitions. She welcomed the new challenge. So Doug and Teri agreed to let Shawn compete in gymnastics for as long as she wanted.

Several weeks later, Teri and Doug sat in the stands watching their daughter prepare for her first meet. In a sea of older girls, tiny Shawn Johnson stood out among the competitors. Her parents worried. Had they made the correct decision? Would their daughter be devastated if she did not finish high in the standings?

When the meet began, Shawn quickly emerged as the fan favorite. The crowd cheered heartily for the smiley gymnast with endless energy. It was clear the young girl loved gymnastics. The enchanted spectators found themselves clapping and cheering her every move.

In the end, Shawn finished in 12th place. The tiny gymnast missed a few landings and lacked overall polish. Nevertheless, the crowd, enamored with the tiny competitor, loudly booed her final placement.

Teri and Doug, on the other hand, felt thrilled with their daughter's accomplishment. Meanwhile, Shawn had so much fun competing. She couldn't wait to do it again, vowing to continue training and gain new skills. The young girl loved the thrill of competition.

There was no turning back now!

"You can't succeed in something unless you're having fun."

Competing, Competing, Competing!

A crowd of children gathered around the playground area at Westridge Elementary School in West Des Moines, Iowa. Eight-year-old Shawn commanded an audience as she performed a gymnastics routine on the monkey bars while her classmates cheered wildly.

Yes, little Shawn Johnson was now creating quite a roar in her hometown. People outside of her gym had started taking notice of her talent. Her name now appeared semi-regularly in the *Des Moines Register* newspaper whenever she competed at gymnastics meets.

One day a television news crew interviewed Shawn and Chow. The TV station even filmed one of their training sessions.

"It just is a really fun sport for me," Shawn answered, when a reporter asked her why she loved gymnastics. "I don't think I would enjoy soccer, or something, as much as this."

"She can't ever get enough of gymnastics," Chow told the news team.

There are 10 levels of gymnastics, followed by junior elite and senior elite. Levels 1 and 2 are for beginners, and 3 and 4 are widely considered the intermediate stage. 5 through 9 feature competitive gymnastics which become progressively more difficult and demanding with each new level. Once a gymnast reaches level 10, they are just one step away from elite gymnastics, where the athlete can compete in international competitions.

When Doug and Teri first enrolled Shawn in gymnastics class, the couple never expected her to achieve a high level. They just wanted their daughter to have fun and work off some extra energy! Yet Shawn loved the sport so much that she quickly climbed up the levels.

At 11 years old, Shawn competed in level 9 gymnastics and loved every moment of it. The bubbly adolescent now owned a large collection of medals.

At one particular meet in Iowa City, Shawn placed first in the all-around, bars, beam and floor. Not only was the strong competitor happy with her placements, she felt thrilled to compete so well in the city where Chow first lived when he moved to the United States. The young girl adored her coach and enjoyed making him proud.

"He works you hard enough so that you can progress, but at the same time he makes it fun," Shawn told the *Des Moines Register* in 2003.

The burgeoning star sometimes even traveled outside of Iowa to compete. In February of 2003, she and her parents flew to Las Vegas, Nevada, to compete in the Go For It Classic. Shawn blinked her eyes in disbelief when she first arrived in the famous city. Bright, glitzy billboards and flashing lights illuminated the famed Vegas Strip. Hotels with grand themes cluttered the historic street. A hotel modeled after Paris, France, featured a replica Eiffel Tower and another, modeled after Egypt, boasted a great pyramid!

Shawn - Gymnastics Competitor
(Photo by Ricardo Bufolin)

Shawn had traveled to Las Vegas for a competition, though, and she quickly turned her attention back to her sport. Unfortunately, the talented gymnast contracted the flu and had difficulty concentrating during practices for the upcoming meet. During one practice, the young girl felt too weak to even run through her routines.

Soon Shawn's stubborn streak kicked in. She hadn't flown over a thousand miles to withdraw from the competition. At first, Doug, Teri and Chow balked when the plucky gymnast insisted on competing, but she finally convinced them to let her try. The tiny dynamo then resumed her game face, summoning all her concentration for the meet. She left Las Vegas with a gold medal in the all-around, bars, beam and floor; and a silver medal in vault!

After the competition, Chow claimed Shawn gave the gutsiest performance he'd seen an ill athlete give since Michael Jordan's famed flu-ridden performance at the 1997 NBA

Finals. Stricken with a terrible stomach virus, the Chicago Bulls' captain insisted on playing in a crucial game against the Utah Jazz. In one of sport's most memorable moments, the basketball legend, pale and weak, helped his team to an emotional victory that propelled them to win the NBA championship.

Later that month, Shawn traveled to St. Joseph, Missouri, to compete in the Pony Express Challenge. She helped Chow's Gymnastics win the grand champion title, while also placing first in every individual category possible: all-around, vault, bars, beam and floor.

Shawn then flew to Fullerton, California, for her biggest competition to date: USA Gymnastics' Junior Olympics Western National Championships. When the well-traveled competitor arrived in sunny Southern California, she felt more nervous than usual. As a result, she made little mistakes throughout the competition, committing errors on bars, floor and vault.

"It was not her best meet," Chow later told the *Des Moines Register*.

Fortunately, Shawn did not leave the Golden State completely disappointed. When the competition ended, she earned a gold medal on balance beam! A few months later, a few miles down the road in Anaheim, the elite American ladies gymnastics team made history by winning the United States' first ever team gold at a world championship.

It wouldn't be long before Shawn would also make history.

Shawn enjoys a University of Iowa basketball game.
(Photo by Don McLaughlin)

"My other life keeps me calm and grounded and normal."

Family & Gymnastics

Now a level 10 gymnast, Shawn dominated various meets across the country. At the Iowa Girls State meet in Ames, she won gold in every category: all-around, vault, beam, bars and floor. People began talking about her chances of competing in international events someday.

"One more year of preparation and after that she should be able to represent the USA," a pleased Chow told the *Des Moines Register*.

"I just want to try my hardest and see where I get from there," Shawn added modestly.

After many years together, Shawn and Chow forged a special friendship. In fact, she even started referring to him as her second dad. Years earlier, she actually gave him the first competition medal she ever won as a thank you for his guidance.

When Shawn returned home from workouts, though, the Johnson family rarely discussed gymnastics. Her parents even forbid any equipment in the house. When their daughter was home, they wanted her all to themselves.

Shawn was also a tiger now - symbolically speaking. She attended Indian Hills Junior High in Clive, Iowa. The moderately-sized school for seventh and eighth grade students used a tiger as its mascot. Despite Shawn's gymnastics success, her friends treated her like any other girl. They chatted about school, music, boys and shopping. In fact, they rarely discussed gymnastics at all.

Around the same time, Shawn adopted a new Golden Retriever after her previous dog, Duke, passed away. One day, while reading the newspaper, her family discovered a couple that needed a new home for their puppy. The Johnsons quickly

Shawn listens to Coach Chow.
(Photo by Ricardo Bufolin)

volunteered to take the dog. Shawn named her new friend, Tucker. Like Duke, the youngest Johnson adored her pet and took him everywhere with her. One could often find Tucker and Shawn on walks, exercising together or just cuddling up to watch television.

Shawn loved animals in general. Though Chow disapproved, she often went horseback riding with her family. During her spare time, Shawn also volunteered at a local animal shelter where she walked dogs so they could have proper exercise.

If gymnastics hadn't lured the young girl into its spell, Shawn might have found another sport to conquer. For starters, she loved diving, which bears many similarities to gymnastics. Both sports require powerful tumbling ability, extreme flexibility and precise balance.

Shawn also loved track and field. She counted running as one of her favorite activities. Often times she would suit up and take Tucker for a run with her. She even loved running on a track and clearing hurdles.

Like most families, the close-knit Johnsons always looked forward to family vacations. On one occasion the family flew to Walt Disney World Resort in Orlando, Florida. Shawn especially enjoyed her visit to the Magic Kingdom where she counted meeting Minnie Mouse as a top highlight.

Still, Shawn's heart ultimately belonged to gymnastics. So when her final class in the school day arrived, or a family vacation eventually wound down, she always felt that itch to return to Chow's gym for a hard workout. Yes, make no mistake about it. Gymnastics now inhabited a revered place in Shawn Johnson's heart.

"I love performing in front of a crowd. The bigger, the better."

Budding Star

Thanks to a top-four finish at the Junior Olympics, Shawn received an invitation for a four-day visit to the U.S. Olympic Training Center in Colorado Springs, Colorado. A facility for U.S. Olympic and Paralympic athletes, the USOTC, as it's called for short, hosts training camps, provides room and board for many top athletes and features world-class exercise equipment. Shawn enjoyed staying at the prestigious center and attending various instructional classes.

At the same time, the 2004 Summer Olympic Games in Athens, Greece, kicked into full swing. The US ladies took silver in the team event. Plus, Texas native Carly Patterson became the first American woman to win the all-around in a fully attended Olympics.

The individual all-around competition stands as gymnastics' most prestigious title. In the all-around, each competitor competes on every apparatus. The gymnast who then compiles the highest point total in the end wins the all-around title. Past Olympic all-around champions include Nadia Comaneci from Romania, Russian Larisa Latynina and America's Mary Lou Retton.

As the 2004 Summer Olympics wrapped, U.S. sports enthusiasts began searching for the next 'It Girl' in gymnastics.

Which promising American gymnast might win a gold medal at the 2008 Olympic Games in Beijing, China?

One girl who gained much attention at the time? American Nastia Liukin, who like Patterson, lived in Texas and even trained at the same gym. The willowy blonde came from gymnastics' royalty. Her mother, Anna Kotchneva, won a gold and silver medal at the 1987 World Rhythmic Gymnastics Championships in Varna, Bulgaria. Meanwhile, Nastia's father, Valeri Liukin, took home two gold and two silver medals at the 1988 Olympics in men's gymnastics.

Nastia Liukin
(Photo by Getty Images)

At the time of the 2004 Olympic Games, Nastia was already a two-time U.S. all-around champion in the junior division. Unfortunately, due to minimum age requirements established by the International Federation of Gymnastics, the young girl fell a few months shy of qualifying for senior competitions. A frustrated Marta Karolyi, the U.S. Gymnastics National Team Coordinator, even remarked that she would have named Nastia to the 2004 Athens team had she been age-eligible.

All throughout the summer of 2004, Nastia starred in an Adidas TV commercial that received especially heavy rotation during the Olympic broadcasts. In the popular spot, Nastia recreated Nadia Comaneci's famous 1976 Olympic uneven bars routine, while clever film editors spliced old footage of the gymnastics legend also performing the program. The end result gave the illusion that the two gymnasts were performing the routine together – frozen in time.

This popular commercial added much buzz to Nastia's image. Who was this talented young girl too young to compete in Athens? Could she be the next Nadia? Was she gymnastics' future superstar? Nastia quickly became the girl to watch in 2008.

Meanwhile, Shawn remained under the radar, competing at the Junior Olympics (U.S. Level 10) National Championships. She finished fourth in the all-around, first on beam and second on floor. Samantha Peszek, who would someday become Shawn's friend and teammate, finished second in the all-around competition.

Chow also looked ahead to the next Olympics. As a special surprise for his students, one day he arranged for gymnastics legend Shannon Miller to speak at his gym. The Oklahoma native won five medals at the 1992 Barcelona Olympics and captured all-around world titles in 1993 and 1994. At the 1996 Olympics in Atlanta, she and her teammates, dubbed the Magnificent 7, made history by winning America's first women's team gold medal. Shannon then capped off those Olympics with a gold medal on the balance beam. When she officially retired in early 2000, Shannon owned the title as the most decorated gymnast in U.S. history.

Shawn and her training mates sat wide-eyed as they eagerly listened to the Olympic champion talk candidly about her experiences as an elite gymnast. Shannon, who holds a B.B.A. in Marketing and Entrepreneurship from the University of Houston, and a law degree from Boston College, placed a strong emphasis on the importance of education.

When Shannon asked if the young gymnasts had any questions for her, Shawn raised her hand eagerly. She asked her hero for advice on coping with the stress of major competitions, such as the Olympics. Shannon suggested that gymnasts should run through the routines in their head, relax and then take each element at a time. Already a hard worker, Shawn felt her motivation and determination increase even more after meeting an Olympic and world champion!

A year later, Shawn's gymnastics continued progressing rapidly. Chow believed she was as talented as any other 13-year-old in the sport. Her only setback? She trained at a small Midwest gym that most people never heard of.

Chow then brainstormed a bold idea. He videotaped Shawn training and mailed a copy to Marta Karolyi, who, in addition to selecting Olympic teams, helped picked American gymnasts for international assignments. Originally from Romania, Marta, along with her husband Bela, helped place Romanian gymnastics on the competitive map in the 1970s.

Most notably, she and Bela once coached the extraordinary Nadia Comaneci, whom many considered the greatest female gymnast ever. At the 1976 Olympics in Montreal, Canada, Nadia won three Olympic gold medals, including the esteemed all-around event. Four years later, at the 1980 Olympics, she picked up two more gold medals on the balance beam and floor exercise routines. In all, Nadia won nine Olympic medals throughout her amazing career.

Together Bela and Martha trained eight Olympic champions during their career. Other notable gymnasts coached by the legendary Karolyis included: Mary Lou Retton, Keri Strug, Julianne McNamara and Dominique Moceanu.

Marta retired from coaching in the late 1990s and now used her vast experience to work for USA Gymnastics. She and Bela ran a camp from their home in a beautiful getaway surrounded by the Sam Houston National Forest in Texas. The country's best gymnasts were invited to the training camp every few months, where they held training sessions and mock competitions. The Karolyi Camp worked to build camaraderie and healthy competitiveness. Being invited to the prestigious camp meant you had arrived in elite gymnastics.

A slight woman with a thick Romanian accent, Marta was a tough woman to impress. One afternoon, she sat down in her office and popped in the videotape of Shawn that Chow sent. Enclosed he included a note that claimed his gymnast would be beneficial to the U.S. team.

"Wow, this coach is pretty confident," Marta thought, as she pressed the play button on her VCR.

Yet when Marta watched the tape, her eyes widened. The bubbly young gymnast reminded her of another great gymnast from the past - Kim Zmeskal, the first American woman to win gymnastics all-around world title. Marta knew Kim well. She and Bela coached her to that world title and a bronze medal at the 1992 Barcelona Olympics. Little did Marta know that Kim was Shawn's number one idol!

Like Kim, Shawn boasted a sturdy, powerful body with explosive power, steady nerves and complex tumbling skills. Marta needed to see this girl in person. She picked up her phone and dialed Chow's number. When he answered, she only had one message for him.

"Bring this girl to my camp in March," she said.

Shawn - Future Superstar
(Photo by Ricardo Bufolin)

"You have to be committed to your sport and committed to your practice."

The Karolyi Ranch

When Shawn arrived at Marta and Bela's 1,200-acre ranch, she felt extremely nervous. What would it be like spending five days at the camp, working hard alongside other gymnasts?

Shawn had never seen such a grand gymnastics facility in all her life. The training center included a 35,000 square-foot gymnasium complex, an enormous lake for boating, an animal petting zoo, horseback riding and nature trails, an Olympic size swimming pool, cabin dormitories, a soccer field, basketball and tennis courts, a game room and more!

After Shawn soaked up her new surroundings, she scoured the facility for the legendary coach who owned the ranch. Finally after an hour, she spoke up.

"I've been here over an hour and I still haven't seen Bela!" she said.

When Bela heard of this girl inquiring about him, he rushed to meet her. He loved her spitfire attitude and beautiful smile.

Later at the first training session, Bela and Marta watched Shawn carefully. When they looked at her, she reminded them of Kim, Bela's favorite student ever. It felt like a ghost from their past had reappeared many years later, untouched by the passage of time. Unbeknownst to them, Kim was also Shawn's favorite gymnast. As Marta stood watching Shawn train at her camp, a nickname popped into her head. Kimbo II.

It was no surprise that Bela quickly developed a fondness for Shawn. She possessed Kim's muscular build, explosive gymnastics and captivating performance skills.

"In my 40 years of coaching, I never saw two individuals more alike," he later told *Sports Illustrated*.

As luck would have it, Kim, who now owned a gym of her own, lived nearby. One day she stopped by the training camp for a visit. Shawn eagerly cornered Kim for several minutes and bombarded her with questions, which her hero happily answered.

It wasn't all work at the camp, though. Shawn quickly became friends with other gymnasts. When they finished training for the day, they hung out in their rooms and styled each other's nails, makeup and hair, or spent time on the Internet.

"I love training here," she told a reporter. "Being in the middle of the forest takes you away from the distractions of home. It adds to the experience of being focused on just gymnastics."

Of course, Shawn still had homework every day. Some of the older gymnasts helped her when she struggled with an assignment. Sometimes she emailed questions to her teachers.

When the camp finally ended, Shawn felt a little sad. She made friends, met several gymnastics legends and enjoyed the intense training sessions. Judging by Bela and Marta's enthusiastic response to the young gymnast, though, Shawn would return to the camp again soon.

Shawn - Pan Am Games
(Photo by Ricardo Bufolin)

"I always have fun. I love what I do and I love my sport and it shows. I hope they think of me as the smiley one."

National Team Member

Now a junior elite gymnast, Shawn felt thrilled when she was invited to compete at the U.S. Classic. A major competition, the senior portion of the event was broadcast on television.

With such a prestigious competition on her daughter's schedule, Teri realized that Shawn was now a top gymnast. The tumultuous path ahead would be difficult and paved with many sacrifices. The loving mother couldn't help but worry for her little girl. Teri needed confirmation that Shawn truly wanted to pursue her sport for the unforseeable future. One day she sat her daughter down for a serious talk and asked her if she really wanted to head down the challenging road.

"Mom, I love it," Shawn answered sincerely.

After hearing her daughter's response, Teri relaxed. Shawn had made it clear that gymnastics was her choice. She would continue to support her daughter the best that she could.

When Shawn arrived in Virginia Beach, Virginia, she marveled at the beautiful city. A popular resort destination, the town featured stretches upon stretches of beaches, hotels, restaurants and retail stores.

When Shawn walked into the gigantic Virginia Beach Pavilion Convention Center, she wore a royal blue leotard with silver sequins. Her hair was pulled back into several delicate twists and capped off with a ponytail. She looked around at her

Shawn waits to compete.
(Photo by Tomas Tyrpekl)

fellow competitors. She had watched some of the girls on television and now she would compete against them. In fact, there were television cameras everywhere!

Meanwhile, the senior women's competition included gymnastics' newest star, Nastia Liukin, who won the all-around event. World team member Jana Bieger, Alicia Sacramone, a stellar vaulter, and Chellsie Memmel, then a two-time world champion, finished second, third and fourth, respectively.

Shawn vowed to make a good impression on all the gymnastics folks there, especially Marta. She wanted people to know she belonged at the competition and could contend with the country's best junior gymnasts.

In the end, Shawn enjoyed a terrific meet. She won the bronze medal in the all-around and another bronze on the balance beam. She also placed fifth on floor and vault and ninth on the uneven bars. Most importantly, her top-three finish qualified her for the 2005 U.S. Gymnastics Championships!

By the time Shawn left Virginia Beach, she had generated much buzz. Many asked questions about the talented girl who seemingly came out of nowhere to medal in the junior all-around. Some gymnastics experts compared her work on the balance beam to Olympic champion Carly Patterson! Marta even listed Shawn as a young gymnast with a shot at making the 2008 Olympic team!

Shawn couldn't believe it. People now mentioned her as a gymnast with a great chance at competing at the Beijing Olympics. How had this happened? After all, she had begun competing in gymnastics just for the fun of it!

When Shawn returned home, she began training for the U.S. Championships. If she finished in the top 15, she would make the national team and become eligible for international competitions.

Prior to U.S. nationals Shawn told the *Des Moines Register*, "I am really getting nervous for the championships, but I'm trying not to think about it. I'm going to go into the meet just thinking it's a regular meet. I'll try to do my best."

Shawn, her coaches and parents then traveled to Indianapolis, Indiana, to compete at her first national championships. Conseco Fieldhouse, home to the NBA's Indiana Pacers, hosted the competition.

Unfortunately, Shawn got off to a rough start on the first day of competition. Although the young teenager performed well on her vault and uneven bars routine, she had uncharacteristics falls on her floor exercise and beam. At the end of the night, she found herself in a distant 13th place.

Chow was not upset with Shawn, though. He noticed something very important. Despite making two major mistakes, his student never gave up. She continued to give 100% in the competition. Because of Shawn's unwavering determination, he had strong faith that she would rebound strongly from her disappointing first day.

On the final day of competition, just as Chow anticipated, Shawn fought very hard to overcome her unfortunate deficit. The unflinching competitor recorded especially strong performances on the balance beam and vault. Her efforts moved her up to 10th place overall. Meanwhile, a strong bars worker from Houston, Texas, Natasha Kelly, won the gold medal.

"She bounced back beautifully," Chow raved. "It was a great learning experience."

"I just really wanted to make the (national) team," Shawn remarked happily. "Now that I have, I'm just overwhelmed."

Shawn warms up.
(Photo by Ricardo Bufolin)

"The sky's the limit. You can do anything and go anywhere if you put your heart into it."

International Competition

Charleroi, Belgium. Shawn would fly to the historic city for her first international competition. She was representing the United States at the Top Gym competition. Girls from eight different countries were set to compete against one another. The focused athlete trained very hard for the competition, determined to represent her country to the best of her ability.

Shawn felt very excited to travel to Belgium. Never before had she stepped out of the country. Would she experience jet lag? What kind of food would they serve in Belgium? Would she like it?

From the moment Shawn stepped on the competitive floor in her adorable red and white leotard, the crowd loved her. In particular, they adored her floor routine to Belinda Carlisle's '80s hit, "Heaven is a Place on Earth." Enchanted by Shawn's infectious smile and obvious love for the sport, the audience clapped along enthusiastically to her music and cheered loudly for her dynamic tumbling.

When the competition ended, Shawn became the proud owner of several medals! She won the all-around title, vault and floor exercise. Three times she stood on the medal podium as officials draped a gold medal around her neck. Each time she smiled proudly with her hand over her heart as her country's national anthem played and organizers raised the American flag.

When Shawn returned to Des Moines, the media attention surrounding her intensified. In fact, her star had risen all across the country. Gymnastics followers from around the country now knew Shawn Johnson's name!

"To think that I'm actually known as an international gymnast now is kind of scary," Shawn remarked. "Knowing that I'm seen all over the world is a lot different. It's a big step for me."

Shawn didn't travel very far for her second international meet. She flew to Houston, Texas, for the USA/Japan/New Zealand Competition. As fate would have it, the all-around competition fell on her birthday, and she won! She followed up her big victory with four medals in the remaining four events: gold in vault and balance beam, silver on floor exercise and third on the uneven bars.

A few weeks later, Shawn attended her third international of the year, the 2006 Pacific Alliance, in gorgeous Honolulu, Hawaii. She fell in love with the beautiful state the moment she stepped off the plane. In fact, it quickly became her favorite travel destination. In particular, Shawn loved the tranquil beaches and warm tropical climate.

The 2006 Pacific Alliance featured gymnasts from 15 countries. Shawn dominated the competition. She left the event with gold medals in the all-around, vault, floor and uneven bars. She also nabbed the silver medal on the balance beam.

Despite Shawn's strong showings all season, success never went to her head. Always a good sport, she lavished high praise on her competitors.

"The Chinese are very strong," Shawn remarked honestly. "A Chinese girl beat me on beam in Hawaii. She's better."

Though she had racked up an impressive collection of medals, Shawn never let up in her training. She continued working hard at the gym every day. Shawn liked surprising judges with new skills. It gave her great pride to learn fresh elements.

When she arrived at the 2006 U.S. Classic in Kansas City, Missouri, Shawn felt determined to try a daring new skill on the floor exercise. At the end of her first tumbling pass, she landed a double-double - two back flips with two twists. Shawn's feat made her the first American woman to complete such a difficult element!

Shawn's achievement received much excitement in Kansas City. Among those impressed? Marta Karolyi.

"She's one of the most promising girls coming up when we think about the 2008 Olympics," Marta gushed to the *Des Moines Register*.

"It's not just the physical aspects that are impressive," Marta continued. "She's got that mental capacity. She's very determined. She has very high goals set, and she also realizes she has to match effort with the goals."

Next Shawn looked ahead to the 2006 U.S. Gymnastics Championships. Thanks to her victories at U.S. Classic and other international meets, she entered the competition as a strong favorite to capture the junior all-around title. Would Shawn rise to the challenge?

"I can't control what scores they give me. I can only control my routines and how I do."

2006 U.S. Championships – Junior Division

Shawn credited her amazing season in large part to Chow's supportive coaching. To thank him for his valuable guidance, she had her name stitched in Chinese characters on her leotard.

The 2006 U.S. Gymnastics Championships were held in picturesque Saint Paul, Minnesota, a mere four-hour drive from West Des Moines. The city's close proximity to Shawn's hometown meant that many of her friends and family could make the drive to see her compete.

All eyes rested on Shawn when she entered the Xcel Energy Center, a four-level arena in the heart of downtown. Not once did the heavy favorite flinch under the enormous expectations. At the end of the all-around competition, she won the gold with a score of 124.100. That was nearly four points higher than the silver medalist, Bianca Flohr. In fact, Shawn's score was so strong, it would have placed first in the senior girl's division too, which Nastia Liukin won!

An emotional Kim Zmeskal sat in the arena observing Shawn carefully. The former world champion bit her lip and held back tears as she watched Shawn cruise to the junior title. Like so many others, she, too, noticed a strong resemblance between the two gymnasts.

"I feel very fortunate to have been around her for almost two years," Kim told *Sports Illustrated*. "She's a super-fierce competitor. There definitely is a connection, but I'm almost timid to say it because I'm complimenting myself."

When reporters and other media folks gathered to interview Shawn, they mentioned her resemblance to Kim. Shawn acknowledged her hero but also stressed that she brought her own unique qualities to her gymnastics.

Kim Zmeskal
(Photo Courtesy *Time*)

"She's my favorite gymnast," she told *Sports Illustrated*. "But I never tried to copy her."

Later at the medal ceremony, Shawn encountered another gymnastics legend. 1984 Olympic All-Around Champion Mary Lou Retton placed the gold medal around her neck!

"It was really cool," Shawn later told *Sports Illustrated*. "It was overwhelming to have her give me my gold medal."

Shawn wasn't done winning medals, though. She won three more gold medals in event finals: vault, balance beam and floor. She also captured a silver medal on the uneven bars. Incidentally, Shawn's floor exercise score would have won gold in the senior competition.

With the junior all-around gold medal in her possession, Shawn now looked ahead to a senior career. From now on, she would compete against Olympic and world competitors! Many in the gymnastics community believed she had already booked her ticket to the 2008 Olympics!

"She's a little spitfire," Mary Lou remarked. "She reminded me of myself 20 years ago. She's a little image of me. She's got the full package -- powerful and energetic. She has that smile and everybody loves her. She's definitely going to be in Beijing."

"I'm a perfectionist. Every little detail matters."

Senior Gymnast

Shawn Johnson – Senior Elite Competitor. Little Shawn Johnson who began gymnastics just for fun was now one of the top gymnasts in the United States. She would be eligible to represent her country in major competitions like the world championships and the Olympic Games!

In March of 2007, Shawn attended her first major senior competition: the Tyson American Cup in Jacksonville, Florida. China, Canada, United States and Russia sent talented representatives to this important event.

Though Shawn began the season as a first-time senior, she already garnered a strong following. As a matter of fact, she was quickly becoming one of the sport's biggest stars!

"What's amazing is that the gymnastics fans who have come here to Jacksonville know all about her," *NBC* commentator Al Trautwig remarked. "You can hear it from their reaction when she is introduced."

Now that she competed on the senior level, cameras followed Shawn everywhere. After all, countries all over the world broadcast the competition!

In the end, Shawn won the competition over the reigning U.S. senior silver medalist, Natasha Kelly. She completed four solid routines en route to the title.

After Shawn completed her final program, the floor exercise, she ran to Chow and hugged him tightly. Standing by her coach's side? Marta Karolyi.

"Very nice work," Marta praised, as she, too, offered a big bear hug to the new American Cup champion.

When a reporter questioned Shawn about her reaction to her victory, she used only one word: overwhelming.

"I just went out there, had fun and tried to do my best, and I did," she later explained.

Following her major victory, Shawn began receiving endorsement offers. That is, several companies offered her money to pitch their products for them. If Shawn accepted such monetary deals, she would become a professional athlete.

Being paid to endorse products appealed to Shawn. After all, her parents poured thousands of dollars into her training over the years. Why shouldn't they reap some financial rewards for it?

There was one catch, however. Most elite gymnasts receive full scholarships from colleges in exchange for competing for a university. To compete at the college level, one cannot make money through their sport. If Shawn accepted endorsement money, she would become ineligible to compete in college gymnastics.

After much thought and careful consideration, Shawn elected to turn professional and accept cash prizes and endorsement offers. That didn't mean she wouldn't attend college, though. She still dreamed of attending an Ivy League school and majoring in medicine. Except now, instead of accepting a sports scholarship from a college, she would use the endorsement and prize money to pay her own way through school.

Turning pro let Shawn accept a Coca-Cola endorsement deal.

Four months later, the American Cup champion flew to Rio de Janeiro for the Pan Am Games, where she helped the United States win the team gold. Shawn also won the all-around, bars and beam titles and nabbed silver on the floor.

When Shawn arrived home at Des Moines International Airport, she received a great surprise. Gym teammates, family, friends and television crews waited for her with congratulatory signs. They erupted into hearty applause and presented her with flowers and balloons.

"It was so great because they're like my sisters and my family," Shawn told a reporter. "To see them there welcoming me home…it was overwhelming. I loved it."

"It was the best competition I'd ever been to…the biggest," she added. "I got to meet some of the nicest girls and I had fun."

"I've always wanted to stay the same Shawn Johnson I've always been. And I still feel that way: like a small town girl from Des Moines!"

2007 U.S. Championships

Undefeated all season long, most people expected Shawn to win her first senior national title easily. Everyone that is, but Shawn.

"I still feel like the baby of the group," she insisted before the competition. "I'm the newcomer. I really don't have a title to defend. I'm just earning it and trying to work for it."

In mid-August, Shawn arrived in San Jose, California, to compete at the 2007 Visa Championships. The crowd at the HP Pavillion went wild when they first spotted Shawn on the competition floor. Of course, they also cheered heartily for the reigning national champion, Nastia Liukin. All in attendance, and those watching on television, anticipated an exciting competition between the two girls.

Wearing a flashy white leotard with pink, yellow and orange flames, Shawn hit every routine beautifully. In particular, her balance beam routine drew high praise.

"She has the most difficult beam routine planned in the championships," former Canadian champion and *NBC* commentator, Elfi Schlegel, raved. "I have to say, it's probably the most difficult routine in the world."

After day one, Shawn sat in first place. In fact, she held a big lead over all her competitors. Always levelheaded, she refused to lose focus.

"We still have a whole other day and a whole other event in front of us," Shawn stressed.

When asked how she handled her nerves, she admitted

Shawn and Cyndi Lauper
(Photo by Jamie Lantzy)

that competing at her first senior nationals felt very nerve-wracking - even if she didn't show it.

"I tried to stay calm and tried to hide it and have fun," she explained.

On day two of the all-around competition, Shawn sported an orange and black leotard. She began her evening on the balance beam and flaunted her nerves of steel.

"She looks like she's on the floor," Elfi raved.

Shawn kept her cool throughout the remainder of the competition. At the end of the night, she won the senior all-around gold medal, defeating silver medalist Shayla Worley by over three full points. Nastia, who held the title two years in a row, slipped to third place.

Shawn had much fun competing at nationals. In fact, she enjoyed hanging out with her fellow competitors. After Shawn finished her final routine, she sat on the lap of her friend, Alicia Sacramone, and watched the end of the competition.

"It's funny to watch her because she looks so mature and centered and focused," Alicia commented to the *Associated Press*. "Then when you get her out of the gym, she really is that, a kid. It's so much fun to see her in both worlds."

"I feel like I'm in a dream," Shawn answered, when asked about winning the national title. "I'm always asking for people to pinch me because it never feels real."

"I just came here and wanted to have fun, of course," she continued. "I just wanted to do what I do at home in practice and hit my routines, and I did! I never imagined this."

Shawn then added, "To be here and win is a dream come true."

"If I can motivate some little girl or boy to get into a sport and be active and follow their dreams then I've done my job."

2007 World Championships

It came as little surprise when USA Gymnastics named Shawn to the world team. Shayla Worley, Nastia Liukin, Alicia Sacramone, Ivana Hong and Samantha Peszek were also selected for the squad.

Though she quickly became the favorite for the world all-around title, Shawn admitted to feeling jittery about the competition. She had never competed at such a major event in all her life.

"It's kind of scary," Shawn admitted. "I'll be competing against people I watched on TV last year. You just have to go out there and keep your blinders on."

Stuttgart, Germany, played host to the 2007 World Gymnastics Championships. Shawn's competition would begin with the team event. The American girls were favored to take the title.

Besides combatting jet lag, Shawn, an only child, dealt with the difficulty of sharing a room with two other teammates, Ivana and Bridget. Though the girls loved one another dearly, their differences were obvious. Shawn needed complete silence while she slept. Meanwhile, Bridget slept with the lights, TV and computer on. She even left the shades wide open!

"How do you do it?" an incredulous Shawn asked Bridget.

On the day of the qualifying round, the girls put their minor differences aside and pulled together to take the lead by a wide margin, nearly four points. The team competed brilliantly that day. In particular, Shawn performed a stellar beam, Nastia rocked her bars set and Alicia owned the vault.

On the final day of team competition, the day when medals were awarded, Marta selected Shawn as the only American gymnast to compete on all four events. Her decision showed her strong faith in the new U.S. champion.

Unfortunately, the American women seemed a bit wobbly on the second day. Nastia Liukin, normally an excellent balance beam worker, lost her concentration during her routine and fell off the apparatus on the simplest gymnastics move. She threw her hand over her head in horror and disbelief. The gaffe cost Team USA almost .60 of a point.

Shawn followed her teammate, knowing she needed a great performance. However, she appeared distracted throughout her program, and she, too, fell off the balance beam. Shawn looked dazed by her uncharacteristic error.

With one event remaining, the teammates sat despondent when they fell to second place in the standings. Ever the optimist and fighter, Shawn looked at the scoreboard and immediately began calculating numbers.

"We're only .01 out of first place," she excitedly told her teammates.

Suddenly, the Americans stopped sulking. Their faces brightened and their bodies snapped to attention. They could still win the team gold medal.

Alicia, the team captain, gathered her teammates in a big circle. She gave them the pep talk of their life. The motivated girls cheered when she finished speaking and walked confidently to their final event, the floor exercise.

Shayla Worley led off for the United States. She performed a somewhat solid routine with a few shaky landings. However, she scored lower than the team hoped.

Shawn competed next and hit every element in her program. In particular, her tumbling passes were a standout. As she performed her floor exercise with plucky abandonment, Shawn could not contain her beaming smile.

"Boy, is she in her element now," remarked Olympic champion Bart Conner.

She ran off the floor beaming and high-fived Alicia. Then the thrilled gymnast hugged all of her teammates tightly.

"I knew I needed to make up for beam," Shawn later told the *Los Angeles Times*. "I was proud I could do that."

Right before Alicia began her program, Shawn shouted encouragement to her teammate, "You got it, Alicia!" The other American girls also cheered on the veteran gymnast.

In the end, Alicia delivered a magnificent routine and perhaps the most exciting floor exercise of her career. Before she finished the program, the crowd roared with delight.

Meanwhile, Marta jumped up and down as she pumped her fists in the air. Alicia bit her lip to fight back happy tears as she ran off the floor exuberantly. Many later described Shawn and Alicia's performances as the best back-to-back floor routines ever seen at a world championship!

When Alicia's score came up on the scoreboard, it was high enough to clinch gold for Team USA. American coaches and team officials embraced excitedly, while the women's team, who'd grown close so quickly, enjoyed a celebratory group hug.

Team USA - World Champions
(Photo by Tomas Tyrpekl)

Moments later, Shawn and her teammates stood proudly on the podium representing the red, white, and blue. After their national anthem played, they raised their flowers triumphantly while gold medals sparkled around their necks. For the rest of their lives, Shawn and her teammates would be called world champions.

"I never saw myself as the 'It Girl.' I never saw myself as having all the talent. I loved being in the gym and that was it."

2007 World Championships: The All-Around Competition

Shawn had little time to celebrate the United States' team victory. Days later, she returned to the arena for the all-around competition. She and Nastia were the top two American gymnasts to qualify.

Wearing a shiny blue leotard with silver sequins, Shawn began her competition on the vault apparatus. She performed a risky Yurchenko double and nailed it. She was off to a great start! At the end of round one, she stood in third place with three rotations to go.

For her second apparatus, Shawn would battle the uneven bars. She completed a strong routine and stuck her landing. Chow grinned with delight when she approached him. He felt quite proud of his young student.

"You just look at her and you feel calm," Olympic gold medalist Tim Daggett raved.

Midway through the competition, Nastia led the international field. Meanwhile, Shawn sat in fifth place, but she would finish the championship on her two best events: balance beam and floor exercise.

Shawn felt nervous heading into her beam routine. She had made a mistake on the apparatus during team finals. Could she hold it together during the all-around competition?

Nearly halfway through her beam routine, Shawn attempted the same element she fell on during the team final. She nearly fell off the apparatus again but saved herself from falling.

"That's really the mark of a veteran, and yet she's new to major international competition," Bart Conner praised. "She shows a lot of maturity, and she is fearless out there. She seems to attack regardless of the situation."

Meanwhile, Nastia struggled when it came time for her beam program. She fell off the apparatus yet again. With that mistake, she dropped out of first place and out of the top three entirely.

As Shawn walked to her final event, the floor exercise, the updated standings showed she sat in second place. The gold was firmly within her reach.

After Shawn warmed up, she looked to the only coach she'd ever known for guidance.

Chow told her calmly, "Do your floor and you can win the gold."

Once on the floor, Shawn had the time of her life. After she landed her difficult double-double in her second tumbling pass, her face lit up with joy. When her program ended, Shawn jumped to her feet with youthful enthusiasm. Then she scanned the crowd for her mother and father. The proud daughter wanted to share the moment with her loving parents.

Shawn paced as she waited for the judge's marks. When her score of 15.425 flashed on the scoreboard, Chow hugged his pupil with delight.

Shawn Johnson - 2007 World All-Around Champion
(Photo by Tomas Tyrpekl)

"Congratulations," he told her. "You're the world champion."

Shawn smiled non-stop at the medal ceremony. She hugged her competitors sincerely and congratulated them. Steliana Nistor from Romania won the silver medal, and Brazil's Jade Barbosa and Italian Vanessa Ferrari tied for third place. The new world champion placed her hand over heart as the American national anthem boomed throughout the arena. Tears clouded the young girl's eyes.

"It feels amazing to hear your own anthem," Shawn later remarked. "It makes you really proud. So it was a great feeling."

Afterwards the media asked Shawn how it felt to win the all-around competition.

"I didn't expect to become an elite. To be here today, and to be a senior and having accomplished so many things, it's a dream come true," she gushed. "I feel like all the hard work's paid off."

When questioned on her ever-present smile, Shawn simply answered, "I have fun. I love it, and I think it shows."

However, Shawn's smile broke down when she and her parents reunited after the competition. A proud Doug and Teri wrapped their arms around their daughter, expressed their pride and assured her that everything had truly happened. She was indeed world all-around champion. An emotional Shawn broke down and shed tears of happiness. She felt so grateful to have been blessed with wonderful parents who always supported her.

Having come so close to the all-around title, Nastia felt absolutely devastated. Nevertheless, she displayed her usual class act.

"It's a little disappointing just knowing that, if I didn't have that mistake, I was probably able to place in the top three," she said tearfully. "So I'm just replaying that over in my mind."

"I'm really excited for Shawn," she added. "It's great to see someone like that. It's great to know she's on your team, especially with the Olympics coming up."

Shawn's individual gold medal placed her in some impressive company. She joined Kim Zmeskal, Shannon Miller and Chellsie Memmel as the only American women to win the all-around title at a world championship.

A few days later, Shawn added a third gold medal to her impressive resume when she won the floor exercise in team finals. Incidentally, teammate Alicia Sacramone took the silver medal.

The conclusion of the world championships marked the end of Shawn's first senior season. She had remained undefeated all year in the all-around competition. Make no mistake about it, Shawn established herself as a strong contender at next year's Beijing Olympics.

"The media is always looking for the next "It" Girl," Bart Conner stated in regard to the new three-time world champion. "Well guess who's it?"

"None of this seems real to me. It all seems like a dream. Someone pinch me because I have no idea how I'm a world champion and I'm 15 years old."

A Celebrity

As Shawn sat in an airplane headed for Des Moines, Iowa, one thought consumed her mind. High school. As an honor roll student, Biology, French, Modern American Literature and Geometry comprised her schedule.

Surely her classmates now knew of Shawn's gymnastics background. Newspapers across the country splashed her image on their front page. In fact, *USA Today* called her America's new queen of gymnastics, while *ABC News* named her their Person of the Week!

With the Beijing Olympics less than a year away, major corporations bombarded Shawn's agent with endorsement offers. Many companies wanted the three-time world champion to pitch their products.

When Shawn returned home, though, she spent her time like any normal teenager. Nothing made her happier than spending a quiet day with her parents and dog, Tucker, and cats, Max and Vern. She cherished family time. When Shawn snuggled into her bed at night, she sighed happily. After a long season on the road, she cherished the comfort of her own bed.

Still, when Shawn returned to the gym, she never let up on her training. On her first day back at Chow's, she began working on new skills. As the reigning world all-around champion, people looked to Shawn as the new standard in technical ability, and she intended to raise the bar.

Shawn received a huge honor when the U.S. Olympic Committee announced she and cycling's Brian Lopes had won

got milk?

Flip over it.

Milk. It keeps me fit, inside and out, upside down and right side up. Talk about the perfect balance.

body milk.

Shawn flips for milk.

its September Athletes of the Month. With her world team-mates, she also won the USOC Co-Team of the Month, along with the U.S. Greco-Roman Wrestling Team.

With the Olympics eleven months away, many wondered if Shawn might turn to private tutoring so she could increase her training time. However, she and her parents balked at the idea. Shawn loved attending public school. She had no intention of leaving Valley High School.

"I love public school---always have," she explained. "It's the only social life I get. I treasure it a lot. It's just a break for me from the whole gymnastics scene."

For the remainder of the year. Shawn trained hard while also enjoying the perks of becoming a newfound celebrity. Brodkey's, a local jewelry store, presented her with a custom-made necklace in the shape of the Olympic rings. They created the stunning work from emeralds, rubies, sapphires, onyx and diamonds. With her parents standing next to her, the new world champion even dropped a puck at a home game of the Iowa Stars, a professional hockey team.

On one exciting occasion, Shawn flew to Los Angeles to appear as a guest on comedian Ellen DeGeneres' talk show. When she arrived at the studio, a makeup artist and hairdresser sat in her in a chair and prepared her for the show!

Moments later Shawn walked onto the sound stage in her Team USA warm-up suit. The friendly talk show host asked her how gymnastics first caught her eye, and how it felt to win the world championships. She was also asked about her life outside gymnastics.

"I went to Homecoming," Shawn smiled. "I go to movies and shopping. I guess I'm normal."

Meanwhile back home in West Des Moines, people often asked Shawn's parents if they were traveling to Beijing to watch their daughter compete at the Olympics. More than anything, Doug and Teri hoped to be there in China, but the modest-income family had financially supported Shawn's dream for years. They might not be able to afford such a trip.

Fortunately for the Johnsons, Homesteader's Life, a funeral insurance funding provider, raised $35,000 dollars to send the family to the Olympics! Teri had worked at the company for 16 years, and Shawn's Aunt Sue still worked there. The family felt grateful for the support and generous donations.

Shortly afterwards, Shawn experienced a scare that nearly destroyed her Olympic dream. She began having pain in her leg. Doctors discovered a stress reaction in her right shin. Thankfully, because the injury occurred during the offseason, she had sufficient recovery time. The Olympic hopeful wore a walking boot for two weeks and halted tumbling until it healed.

On October 17, 2000, Iowa Governor Chet Culver declared "Shawn Johnson Day" across the state. With her parents and coaches by her side, the world and U.S. champion stood in the atrium of the Iowa State Historical Building before hundreds of proud Iowans as the governor paid tribute to her.

"Shawn Johnson is an amazing young woman," said Governor Culver. "Her awards and honors are many, and I congratulate her for all she has done in her 15 short years. She is a role model for thousands of girls in Iowa and millions more around the country and the world. I am proud that she represents herself, her family, her state and her nation with grace and dignity. We wish her the best of luck as she heads to Beijing, China, for the 2008 Summer Olympics."

Shawn promotes Coca-Cola.

"Everything that's happened to me is so overwhelming," Shawn remarked in her thank you speech. "I thank Governor Culver for proclaiming today 'Shawn Johnson Day.' It's such a huge honor, and I am grateful that so many people came out to celebrate with me. I'm so proud to be from Iowa!"

As an added bonus, Governor Culver read a letter to Shawn from Lance Armstrong, one of her favorite athletes. The seven-time Tour de France champion congratulated the teenager on her hard work and competitive success.

After the festivities, Adidas, an official sponsor of USA Gymnastics and the 2008 Beijing Olympics, announced a major contract with Shawn. She became the new face of the sports apparel company!

"What better day to announce our partnership with Shawn than on 'Shawn Johnson Day?' We are thrilled to welcome her to the Adidas family," explained Martyn Brewer, Director of Sports Marketing, Adidas America. "Shawn's dedication and humility is an inspiration to athletes around the

Shawn and McDonald's encourage exercise.

Shawn Johnson celebrates the Happy Meal.

world. She embodies everything that is good in sport and her story exemplifies the 'Impossible is Nothing' spirit."

Brewer added, "When you see that smile, you want to be part of it!"

Not to be outdone, Coca-Cola also inked a deal with the gymnastics superstar. Shawn became one of six Olympic hopefuls featured on various Coke products leading up to the Beijing Games. The other esteemed athletes chosen for the campaign? Swimmer Natalie Coughlin, NBA's LeBron James, Tae Kwon Do competitor Steven Lopez, Triathlete Andy Potts, and Sanya Richards, a track & field star.

Shawn's whirlwind endorsement deals also extended to a company with local roots. One afternoon, she filmed a commercial for Hy-Vee, a Midwest supermarket chain. Meanwhile a local car dealer gave her a new red Land Rover LR2 as a birthday present!

Despite her many duties as a spokesperson, Shawn never allowed her ego to inflate. She still remained her usual modest self.

Shawn Johnson - Got Milk Spokesperson

"It is kind of crazy to think that they all want me," the world champion remarked modestly. "I don't see why. But I'm proud and honored."

One day Shawn went grocery shopping with her mother. When she walked down the aisle, what did she find? A cardboard cutout of herself advertising Coca Cola! The embarrassed teenager fled from the store, worried that others might think she shopped at the supermarket just to admire her advertisement.

Shawn would have to become accustomed to seeing her image everywhere. She was the face of women's gymnastics. With the Olympics only months away, the public interest would only intensify!

"I want to be my own person. I want to make history just being me."

Olympic Buildup

The Olympic season kicked off with the Tyson American Cup on March 1st. One competitor, in particular, felt eager to begin the competitive year.

"I'm ready to compete, to get back into the swing of things," Shawn told the *Des Moines Register*.

"I'm pretty sure there's going to be more competition out there just because now I am the one to beat," she continued. "I realize that. I accept that. But I'm still out there to try to beat myself, basically. I'm still working to get even better."

If anything, Shawn thrived on pressure. She actually enjoyed the onslaught of nerves and adrenalin rush that competing delivered. The focused teen believed that they helped her perform better in the long run.

New York City's Madison Square Garden played host for the 2008 Tyson American Cup. So many historic moments occurred at the famed arena. Muhammad Ali boxed there. Michael Jackson performed a concert in it. The Grammy Awards were held there, as were NHL and NBA finals.

At this pressure-packed competition, Shawn would face rival and friend, Nastia Liukin, whom most believed would be her biggest obstacle toward all-around gold in Beijing. The media had already begun drumming up a rivalry between the two gymnasts.

After a particular training session for the competition, Shawn stopped to grant a reporter a short interview. Standing a few feet away, a mother with two little girls watched the gymnastics star carefully. When the question and answer session ended, she flagged down Shawn,

"Please, can you sign for my girls?" Mary Lou Retton asked.

Yes, Mary Lou and her children were big Shawn Johnson fans! In fact, gymnastics legends Nadia Comaneci and Shannon Miller also flew to New York to watch the sport's first big meet of the year. They, like so many gymnastics fans, were anxious to witness a roster of Olympic hopefuls unveil their new routines and see how the athletes dealt with the big season pressure.

When asked about Shawn's approach toward the Olympic season, Mary Lou told the *The New York Times*, "It's a lot of pressure. This will be the most intense six months of her life."

"She's awesome," she added. "She's got the whole package. She's powerful. She's graceful. She's fun to watch."

Shawn opted to use the early competition to test a new vault, a 2 ½ twisting Yurchenko. Unfortunately, she fell on the skill and later admitted that she had tried too hard to stick the landing.

Shawn rebounded from her early error with a solid bars routine that featured a very difficult mount and even harder dismount, a double-twisting double. She received a very respectable score of 15.625.

Next Shawn moved to the balance beam. She loved this event best. She attacked the apparatus, demonstrating aggressive and dynamic gymnastics.

"I don't think anyone in the world tumbles like her!" Tim Daggett raved.

Finally, Shawn completed the competition on the floor exercise. Yet again, she attempted a new skill by adding a whip to a triple full. Her floor program showcased her mighty tumbling, but it also highlighted the improvements she'd made on her dance skills.

In the end, Shawn won three of four events. However, because of her day one mistake, she finished with the silver medal overall. Nastia took home the gold, while Samantha Peszek finished third.

Shawn and her coach handled her first senior all-around loss with much class by warmly congratulating Nastia. Meanwhile Chow hugged Shawn enthusiastically. His student hadn't won, but she debuted new skills on three of four events. Chow was proud of her. Afterwards, Shawn discussed her second place finish with her hallmark grace and resolution.

"My vault was new this year," she explained. "It was the first time performing it in front of a crowd. I did fall. It happens. It's a new skill. I'll go home and work on it."

"I'm not going into a meet looking just for the gold," she clarified. "I'm coming in here to have fun and do my best. I set the bar high for myself at this meet, and I can only do better from here."

"You can't blame her for that vault," a supportive Marta told the *The New York Times*. "Physically, she's ready to do it. Mentally, not yet. She'll do it in Beijing."

A week later, Shawn traveled to Jesolo, Italy, to compete in another international competition. Her dependable gymnastics helped the U.S. triumph in the team competition. She also took home the all-around title.

On April 14th, Shawn and her teammates attended a media summit in Chicago, Illinois. Hosted by the United States Olympic Committee, the event served as an opportunity for invited press to familiarize themselves with Beijing hopefuls. Shawn and other athletes posed for promotional photos and were interviewed by various news organizations.

As reigning world champions, one reporter asked the American girls about their thought process heading into the Olympics. Did their number one ranking help their confidence?

"We do feel more confident and excited to defend our title," Shawn replied.

"China is our biggest competition, and knowing we are going to their home turf gives us a little bit of pressure," she continued. "We are going to be working harder than ever. During the Pan Am Games in Brazil we had a crowd that was against us, but we worked really hard and got their recognition and cheers at the end."

In early May, with the Olympics three months away, Shawn and her teammates returned to the Karolyi Ranch. The girls trained once again under the watchful eye of Marta and Bela. They worked hard and often.

Shawn looked awe-inspiring in her sessions. She hit all her routines, including the vault that tripped her up at the American Cup. The chatty teenager enjoyed spending time

Shawn Johnson Butter Sculpture
(Photo by Flickr.com/ Gene5335)

with her teammates and cherished the training center's peaceful environment.

Meanwhile, Kim Zmeskal, now a coach, attended the camp with her own student, Chelsea Davis. The ex-gymnast understood the pressure of entering an Olympics as the face of USA Gymnastics. Therefore, Kim kept a watchful, protective eye on Shawn.

"I'm just so hopeful," Kim remarked. "The path she's had is very similar to the one I had. I hope she gets the storybook ending."

A month before the 2008 U.S. Championships, Shawn experienced a setback when she nearly lost her training facility.

Iowa rainfall caused flooding throughout much of the flat state. Treacherous thunderstorms threatened Chow's Gymnastics.

One afternoon Shawn trained inside the facility, while outside, dozens of Iowans, including her father, piled sandbags high in an effort to keep the Raccoon River from destroying the training center. Although Shawn ran outside to help the rescue workers, Chow ordered her back inside the gym to continue training.

"I wanted to help," Shawn later told the *Los Angeles Times*. "All those people were trying to save our gym."

Shawn reluctantly retreated back to the training center. She and Liwen began working on her balance beam routine.

"I could hear the water outside," she recalled. "I just tried not to think about it."

Before long, though, Chow rushed back inside his gym and ordered everyone, including Shawn and his wife, to leave the building immediately. The water level outside had become hazardous.

Shawn and Liwen quickly grabbed their belongings and left Chow's gym. When the pair walked outside, they saw fish swimming in the parking lot!

Chow and volunteers then re-entered his gym. They worked for hours as they moved all the gymnastics equipment to the top floor to keep it safe from the water threatening to flood the center. Sadly, Shawn's father tore a bicep while moving the heavy equipment. Shortly after the work crew cleared out the gym's bottom floor, a foot of water flooded the facility.

With a major competition looming, Chow worried his gymnast might lose precious training time. Thankfully, Iowa State University in Ames, Iowa, came to the athlete's rescue by offering her free use of their gymnastics equipment. For days, Shawn and her coach made a 40 mile trek to the college for her training.

Meanwhile back home, when the rainstorms finally ceased, more volunteers returned to Chow's Gymnastics. Shawn's father, an experienced contractor, spent 2,000 dollars of his own money to buy new wood and install a new floor. Others patched holes in walls, and some people painted night and day.

Her community's generosity was not lost on Shawn. In fact, when asked about it, the levelheaded gymnast dismissed the severity of her training situation, explaining that when people are homeless and suffering, her problem seemed superficial.

Meanwhile, Chow watched in wonderment as perfect strangers worked long hours to return his gym to normal. He felt grateful to have chosen Des Moines as his hometown.

"This community in Iowa has made me feel loving in the heart," he commented. "We didn't even have to ask. The people came out. City council members, gymnasts, their parents, friends. It is a warm feeling to have when you don't feel you are a stranger. You belong."

"I don't think I've ever not gotten nervous. When you work so hard for one special day or routine, you want to perform it better than you ever have. We always say at our gym, 'If you lose the nerves, you lose the sport.'"

2008 U.S Championships

In early June, Shawn arrived in Boston, Massachusetts. The historic city was hosting the 2008 U.S. Gymnastics Championships at the Agganis Arena on the Boston University campus.

It came as no surprise that the media focused heavily on Shawn's attempt at a second straight national title. The focused teenager, however, felt more concerned with testing out her programs and executing them to the best of her ability.

"I definitely want to keep the title, but it's not the most important thing for me to have right now," Shawn claimed. "This is definitely just a test run. I'm certainly out there to make an impression on the committee and Marta, and to build confidence in myself going into the trials and into Beijing."

On the first day of competition, Shawn arrived in a striking, fiery orange and yellow leotard with her initials embroidered on her right sleeve. Her golden hair was pulled back into an intricate braid. She looked every bit the superstar of her sport.

While chalking up in preparation for vault, the same one she fell on at Tyson American Cup, Shawn ran the vault through her head. She wanted to land it successfully this time. Suddenly, Shawn heard her floor music start up. Someone at the controls had hit the wrong button. Rather than become frazzled, the good-natured gymnast laughed off the incident and even relaxed a bit.

When Shawn finally attempted the vault in the competition, she flew through the air effortless. Though she stepped out of her landing, it was still a top-notch effort. The judges awarded her a very strong 16.0!

"I've been dreaming about a vault like that for a long time," Shawn gushed after the meet.

Moments later, Shawn debuted her new floor exercise routine, which she hoped showed a more mature side to her gymnastics. After watching the movie, *August Rush*, she wanted to perform to its soundtrack. The movie inspired her greatly and she hoped the audience would connect with the music as she had. The judges were obviously impressed, issuing her a 16.050 for her performance!

After day one of competition, Shawn stood solidly in first place. She had executed her uneven bars as cleanly as possible, while her tumbling skills and dismount on balance beam were the perhaps the best in the world.

On day two of the championships, Shawn arrived in an elegant black and white leotard and a classic ponytail. By the end of the evening, she might take a second straight U.S. all-around title.

"You can hear it in the crowd. These people love her," Al Trautwig commented during the *NBC* broadcast of the competition.

Yet again, Shawn attempted her difficult vault and completed it perfectly. Her confidence on that apparatus was growing by the minute. She then completed another solid uneven bars routine and an impressive performance on beam. Finally, she ended with floor exercise. All five tumbling passes featured her trademark power.

Although Nastia won the second day of competition, Shawn's hefty score from day one kept her in first place overall. She had done it. Shawn was a two-time U.S. champion. Nastia Liukin took second place, while Chellsie Memmel snatched the bronze medal.

"It feels great to be in this position again," Shawn said after the competition. "I had a really great meet."

Meanwhile back in Iowa, her home state's heart burst with pride. Governor Chet Culver said it best when he proclaimed:

"I want to congratulate Shawn Johnson on winning her second consecutive U.S. gymnastics championship in Boston today. It's a feat few gymnasts have accomplished. Shawn has impressed the world with her masterful skills in the gym as well as the poise and grace that she demonstrates in her everyday life. All Iowans are proud of her achievements, and we look forward to cheering her on in Beijing later this summer."

"Knowing that I will have worked for about 12 years for these games – just making the team would be the biggest honor."

Olympic Trials

Several weeks later, Shawn arrived in Philadelphia, Pennsylvania, for the 2008 Olympic Trials. The top two girls in the all-around event would automatically earn spots on the U.S. Olympic gymnastics team. The remaining gymnasts would fly to the Karolyi Camp, and after a few days of intense training, Marta would name the final four girls to the team.

In an effort to restrain her nerves, Shawn imagined the Olympic Trials as just another competition. However, as she warmed up before the event, the Wachovia Center announcer reminded the audience that two girls would be named to the Olympic team at the end of trials. Shawn felt a mixture of nerves and excitement ripple through her. She felt even more determined to compete to the best of her ability.

Over the course of the two-day trials, Shawn left little doubt that she was prepared for the Olympics. Routine after routine, she showcased her remarkable consistency on the most difficult of skills. On both days, she nailed every single apparatus.

While Shawn competed on her floor exercise, the *NBC* broadcasting team marveled at her improved artistry. They also praised her composure and ability to stick her energetic tumbling passes.

"Phenomenal - one of the most difficult routines being done in the world," Tim Daggett raved. "The highest degree of difficulty of anyone in this meet."

When the 2008 Olympic Gymnastics Trials concluded, Shawn looked up at the scoreboard and smiled with glee. She had won the competition. Shawn, her coach and family could now book their plane tickets to Beijing.

"It's amazing. Its honestly a dream come true," she said, emotionally. "I'm so excited. I'm so honored. I'm the happiest girl in the world right now."

"To finally see my name at the top and have it mean something," she continued. "I'm on the team. It makes everything worth it."

Meanwhile, to no one's surprise, Nastia also claimed a spot on the Olympic team with her second place finish at trials. Together, she and Shawn would guide a strong American women's team in China.

Later that evening, in a special ceremony, a moved Shawn and Nastia stood before thousands of screaming fans as they were named to the team. Steve Penny, President of USA Gymnastics, held a microphone in his hand as he addressed the excited crowd.

"These athletes are shining stars for our country as we head into Beijing for the 2008 Olympic Games," he said. "It's my great privilege and pleasure to introduce two members of the 2008 U.S. Olympic team: Shawn Johnson and Nastia Liukin."

USA Gymnastics' two biggest stars looked at one another in shock and disbelief. Was this really happening?

"We made it," Shawn mouthed to Nastia as they fought back happy tears.

Both girls grinned widely, took a step forward and waved to all in attendance. As the crowd cheered wildly, Shawn and Nastia hugged each other tightly. Their gymnastics may have been a lesson in contrast, but they were good friends who had just realized the same big dream.

Doug and Teri Johnson
(Photo by Ricardo Bufolin)

Before she left the City of Brotherly Love, Shawn acknowledged her biggest supporters: her mom, dad and coaches.

"I love them," she said about her parents, as her voice quivered with emotion. "They're my biggest supporters. They've gotten me through the hardest times."

"I couldn't have gotten here without them," Shawn remarked about Chow and Liwen. "They're my second parents, and I hope I made them proud."

"Funny how the love of a German Shepherd can make my whole day better."

Just a Normal Teenage Olympian

"Beijing is going to be crazy," Shawn remarked. "I don't think anything will actually prepare you for the competition, except just giving it your all and showing up."

Everywhere Shawn went, people talked about the Beijing Olympics. Sometimes she answered serious questions. For instance, many asked Shawn how it felt knowing that Chow and Liwen were returning to their home country thanks to her.

"It makes me really proud to know that I worked hard enough to get (them) back to (their) hometown," Shawn told the *Star Tribune*.

Sometimes, the media asked the new Olympian silly questions. For instance, one reporter wanted to know if she enjoyed Chinese cuisine.

"I love Chinese food. I don't know if I like real Chinese food," she giggled. "But I like American Chinese food a lot."

Shortly before the Olympics, the teen discovered that someone had created a Shawn Johnson butter sculpture that was displayed at the Iowa State Fair, an event that draws around one million people each year. A huge honor that few public figures received, other celebrities immortalized in butter included: Elvis Presley, Tiger Woods and John Wayne.

Shawn was everywhere. It became difficult to pick up a Coke can or McDonald's bag without seeing her image on them. One even witnessed Shawn's influence in the clothing industry, when Adidas embarked on a major campaign with the popular gymnast.

Shawn scored a really exciting endorsement when CoverGirl chose her, Nastia and Alicia Sacramone as their newest celebrity models! It marked the first time that the cosmetics company selected female athletes for a campaign! The three gymnasts joined an exclusive line of famous spokesmodels that included Drew Barrymore, Rihanna and Queen Latifah.

On one occasion, CoverGirl flew all three girls to New York for a photo shoot. Unaccustomed to such a sophisticated photo shoot, the girls goofed around while a photographer snapped photos. In other words, they behaved like typical teenagers, and CoverGirl loved it.

"Shawn, Nastia and Alicia are wonderful additions to the CoverGirl family, representing CoverGirl ideals of both inner and outer beauty," said Esi Eggleston Bracey, Vice President of CoverGirl Cosmetics in North America. "We want to honor their confidence and help them shine in the spotlight. We are thrilled they are lending their beautiful faces to CoverGirl."

In addition to their new glamour roles, Shawn, Nastia and Alicia enjoyed private consultations with Molly Stern, CoverGirl's celebrity makeup artist. The renowned beauty expert worked with the gymnasts to create customized looks to sport during the Olympics and other major events.

"CoverGirl has taken a whole new approach with the athlete," Shawn commented during an appearance on the *Today Show*. "We're trying to be great role models for young teens. We looked up to role models like Drew Barrymore and Rihanna, and it's such an honor to finally have that role ourselves."

Alicia, Shawn and Nastia

With all the media attention, it semed easy to forget that Shawn was just your average teenager. Yet, she enjoyed the same things that most girls her age liked.

One of her favorite books? The *Twilight* series. Yes, she rushed to see the movies when they were released! Her celebrity crush? Channing Tatum. Her favorite movie? *Day After Tomorrow*. Favorite TV shows? *Friends*, *Will & Grace* and *America's Funniest Home Videos*.

Anyone who knew Shawn knew her favorite musical group of all time. She talked about them a lot. The Rascal Flatts.

"They're my favorite," she gushed. "They've always been my favorite. I know every song and every word to every song."

Not many people knew that Shawn possessed a creative flair that extended outside floor exercises. The expressive teenager loved drawing and scrapbooking in her spare time. She even wrote poetry as a way to deal with her ever shifting teenage emotions.

The reigning world champion also owned a domestic side. She particularly relished baking mouthwatering desserts. Her favorite concoctions included cookies, brownies and cakes. She also cooked sometimes. Her specialty? White bean chili.

Of course, Shawn enjoyed other sports besides gymnastics. She loved watching the Tour de France. Meanwhile, football ranked as her favorite spectator sport. She also held a particular affection for the University of Iowa Hawkeyes.

Shawn even mingled effortlessly with her classmates. Sure, she sometimes received curious looks after a major competition aired on TV. After a while, though, the student body forgot about Shawn's high-profile life away from school. Eventually, they regarded her as just another kid cheering on the team at the weekly high school football game. Few batted an eyelash when they spotted the teen socializing with a bevy of friends at the occasional school dance.

Yes, Shawn, the number one ranked gymnast in the world, was still your average girl. Nothing made her happier than throwing on a simple t-shirt and jeans and hanging out with family and friends.

As Shawn once remarked herself, "It's fun to travel, but

Shawn chalks up.
(Photo by Ricardo Bufolin)

I'm just an Iowa girl."

An Iowa girl heading to the biggest competition in the world.

"I think in the past year, I've done a lot of growing up. I've experienced so much. Hopefully I've grown up enough that I can handle the Olympics and take on the world."

2008 Beijing Olympics

At four feet eight inches, Shawn held the record as the shortest U.S. Olympian in Beijing, but she packed a big presence. The moment the gymnastics star, accompanied by her parents and coaches, arrived at Beijing Capital International Airport, reporters and photographers recorded her every move. It would remain that way for the duration of the Olympics.

Chow and Liwen had not visited their homeland in years. They felt proud to return to China as the esteemed coaches of gymnastics' biggest star. They, too, would receive much attention throughout the games.

"It was really cool to be in the Beijing airport and hear Chow speaking Chinese to people," Shawn remarked in awe.

After Shawn adjusted to the 14-hour time change, she explored her new surroundings. She tasted authentic Chinese food but didn't like it. The giddy youngster and her parents also went shopping, searching for souvenirs with Chinese characters on them.

Of course, Shawn also spent time in the Olympic Village. She felt thrilled to meet competitors from all over the world. The outgoing gymnast often introduced herself to famous athletes and asked to take photos with them. After all, she was assembling the best Olympic scrapbook ever.

Incidentally, Shawn and Nastia were assigned as room-mates for the Olympic Games. Many people found their living arrangement interesting since the girls were expected to battle one another for the all-around title. The two Americans always dismissed insinuations of a strained rivalry, though.

Shawn competes in the Olympic team competition.
(Photo by Getty Images)

"It's easy to separate," Nastia insisted. "We've never had a problem."

"When we're in the room and stuff, we're no longer com-petitors," Shawn agreed. "We're teammates and best friends."

Marta Karolyi also stressed that the gymnasts got along swimmingly. She believed their friendly rivalry actually benefit-ted them.

"It's a hearty competition," she commented. "When they're doing their routines, each of them wants to be number one. That's good."

Sportswriters enjoyed pointing out the differences in the two superstars' styles. Shawn was muscular and flashy with dynamic skills. On the other hand, Nastia resembled a ballerina with clean lines, astonishing flexibility and elegant artistry.

"They're so different, but the outcome is the same," Alicia Sacramone remarked. "It's still great gymnastics."

On day one of team practice, both girls wore a shiny pink leotard with matching ribbons in their hair. They looked like sisters.

And for the next few days, they would be sisters. All the American girls carried the same goal. They wanted to honor their country by winning a women's team medal.

"We're just one big family. This is our dream, and this is our life."

Chapter Twenty One
The Team Competition

A formidable group composed the U.S. women's gymnastics team. Chellsie Memmel, Samantha Peszek, Alicia Sacramone and Bridget Sloan joined Shawn and Nastia in Beijing. The girls boasted a combined thirteen world gold medals between them.

The Chinese girls also formed a strong contingent. However, nagging doubts regarding the true age of three of their gymnasts dogged them throughout the games. To compete at the Olympic Games, a gymnast must turn sixteen during that same year. In particular, He Kexin, a remarkable bars worker, received the most scrutiny. Earlier in the year, *Xinhua*, the Chinese government's news agency, and *China Daily* newspaper, both reported the gymnast's age as thirteen. Many speculated that members of China's gymnastics federation falsified He's passport, and possibly those of two other Olympians, to get them on the team and boost their gold medal chances.

It seemed everywhere the Americans went, someone asked them about the Chinese team's age controversy. However, the girls simply smiled and stated they were concentrating solely on their own performances.

Right before the team competition, the American women suffered a serious blow when Chellsie, a former world all-around champion, injured her ankle after jamming it on a tumbling pass during practice. Doctors monitored her carefully and determined that she could compete only on the uneven bars.

Despite losing full use of a valuable team member, the American girls rallied together to stay focused and prepared. They felt determined to keep their spirits high, as they competed in the qualifying round, where the top eight teams advanced to finals, and the top 24 gymnasts continued to the all-around competition.

"We're feeling great as a team. We've been working really close together," Shawn declared. "During all of the practices we cheer each other on, help each other out through the hard times, and take care of the small details. We're like a big family. We couldn't love each other any greater. We just want everyone to go out and do their best, and that will make all of us happy."

On day one of the team competition, energized spectators packed the 18,000-seat National Indoor Stadium. Demand for tickets rose so high that scalping prices climbed by the minute. In fact, some people even began producing counterfeit tickets!

The American girls marched into the stadium in perfect unison. They looked confident and upbeat in their red leotards adorned with a large blue, white and gold star.

One by one, the women began warm-up exercises but more misfortune struck. Suddenly, Alicia heard a popping sound. She watched in horror as her best friend, Samantha, fell to the ground in anguish. The Indiana native twisted her ankle. After doctors examined Samantha, they cleared her for the uneven bars only. All other events were off-limits.

The team immediately became teary eyed. They felt devastated for their friend who had eagerly anticipated a full Olympic experience. The girls gathered together and vowed to perform well for their teammate.

Because Samantha was slated to lead off on floor, Marta now scrambled to shuffle the lineup. Sam sat on a chair, her foot bandaged and propped up, as she rubbed her red eyes while the team scurried to adjust to new start orders.

"There's nothing you can do about it," Samantha later told the *Washington Post.* "I'm just thankful to have such an amazing team behind me that can cover for my little injury."

Saddled with unexpected challenges, the women appeared jittery throughout day one. Chellsie and Nastia counted falls on their uneven bars routines. Meanwhile, Alicia Sacramone also committed a major error by stepping out of bounds during floor.

When the qualifying round completed, the U.S. finished in second place behind China, the home crowd favorites. Meanwhile, Shawn and Nastia qualified for the all-around event by finishing one and two, respectively.

"We have made a few mistakes, but it is preliminary, so we have plenty of time to make up," Shawn declared optimistically. "We're human; we're not robots."

Two nights later, the team finals began. In just a few hours, the final placements would be determined. Most believed the gold medal would come down to China or the United States.

"Both teams are strong," Chow claimed. "The results largely depend on how they perform in the finals."

In the team finals, only three girls per country performed on each apparatus. Shawn would be the only U.S. gymnast to compete in all four events, while a still hurt Samantha would sit out night two entirely.

Sporting red leotards with white trim, the Americans began their evening on the vault. Bridget completed a big, powerful vault that earned a hug from Marta and 15.2 from the judges. Alicia followed with a better performance that scored a 15.675, while Shawn executed the best vault of the bunch for a 16.0.

The Americans focused on the uneven bars next. Despite some minor form issues, Chellsie kicked off the group with a solid bars performance that earned a 15.725. Shawn followed with a score of 15.350. Finally, the United States' best bars worker, Nastia, enjoyed a phenomenal outing that netted a whopping 16.90! Halfway through the team competition, the Americans sat in second place.

The U.S. team next faced the balance beam. After being forced to wait several minutes to start her routine, Alicia seemingly lost her focus as she fell on her mount. She shook her head in disgust but jumped quickly back onto the beam and completed a solid routine, but the damage was done. When she returned to her teammates, she bit her lip and fought back tears as Marta and Chow comforted her. She received a low score of 15.1. Fortunately, Nastia and Shawn answered the pressure with beautiful and difficult beam performances that moved the United States within one point of China with one final rotation left.

In the end, the American women let the team gold slip away on their last event. Alicia fell on a double Arabian during her second tumbling pass. A few moments later, she also stepped out of bounds on another pass. Moments later, Nastia and Shawn, too, ventured out of bounds during their routines.

To the crowd's delight, China took the team gold. The American girls finished a distant second, while the Romanian women snatched the bronze medal.

Later at the medal ceremony, Shawn stood on the second step of the podium alongside her teammates. As the final American girl to receive her medal, she smiled when an official presented her with her new silver memento. She had flown over 6,500 miles to represent her country and received a nifty souvenir for her efforts.

"We're feeling great," Shawn insisted afterwards. "Of course a gold would feel better, but we were very proud of our silver, and we worked really hard for it. We couldn't be any prouder of each other."

"I am not disappointed at all," she continued. "We are human when it comes down to it. We make mistakes. China had a better day today. Give us another day, we could probably come out on top."

"I respect China for what they've done," Shawn added. "They really brought their game today."

"Women's gymnastics gets a lot of attention, but that's also why we love it. People recognize our hard work."

The All-Around Competition

Nastia and Shawn. Shawn and Nastia. For the past year, gymnastics aficionados debated which girl would take home the renowned women's Olympic all-around title. Truth be told, people rarely gave thought to anyone else winning the title. The American duo belonged in a class all their own.

Of course many in the media attempted to create a bitter rivalry between the two girls, but Shawn and Nastia always expressed positive words for one another. They genuinely liked one another and respected each other's gymnastics.

"We always think it's funny," Nastia revealed to the *Associated Press*. "Outside the gym, we're good friends, and lots of people can't see it. When we're on the floor, we have to be serious and focused. Outside the gym, we're just like anybody else."

"We're really good friends, we're really good competitors and we're both really good athletes," Shawn agreed. "I think it's great just because it makes me work really hard and makes her work really hard. We're just helping each other get to a higher level for the team."

"I honestly don't see a huge competition or rivalry between us," she added. "We're friends and always have been."

Chow always insisted Shawn concentrate on her own gymnastics. By focusing on other gymnasts' performances, one could lose their concentration. As a result, Shawn thought only of herself when she approached the all-around competition.

"I have been working really hard and, honestly, I couldn't have put in any more preparation," she claimed. "I want to go out there and do my best and know I gave it everything I had. In the end, that's enough."

The top six qualifiers comprised the same group. Shawn, Nastia and the other four gymnasts began the meet on the vault. As the reigning U.S. champion warmed up, she smiled and waved to various people in the stands.

Finally, officials signaled the start of the competition, and the all-around competition began. Of the gold medal favorites, Nastia went first. She executed a beautiful vault with a perfect stuck landing. Shawn followed with a more difficult vault and assumed the lead over her teammate.

Next they advanced to the uneven bars. Nastia knew she could make up big ground on the uneven bars. She unveiled a beautiful routine with outstanding line, extension and rhythm. Shawn also performed well, but the program lacked her teammate's difficulty. By the competition's midway portion, Nastia overtook her friend in the standings.

Shawn kicked off the next apparatus, the balance beam, while Nastia went last. After encouragment from Chow, Iowa's pride and joy produced a solid balance beam with only a small form break on the landing. When Nastia took her turn on the treacherous beam, she delivered an exquisite routine with no obvious deductions. With one event to go, the elegant Texan held a .6 lead over Shawn.

Nastia took the floor knowing that if she committed no errors, she would win the all-around title. Performing to the Russian folk song, "Dark Eyes," the graceful beauty resembled a ballerina as she tumbled her way to a career best floor exercise.

By the time Shawn took the floor, she had little chance of taking the all-around title. A competitor first and foremost, it didn't stop her from delivering an exceptional floor routine filled with fabulous tumbling that got bigger as the program progressed. When she finished her routine, the audience roared with approval.

"What a way to round up this women's final," *BBC* commentators raved.

Shawn ran over to Chow and hugged him tightly. Then she smiled, waved to the crowd and waited for her score. In the end, she received the same floor exercise mark that her top opponent earned, 15.525, and could not overtake her.

Nastia broke down in tears upon learning she had captured the title. Shawn hugged the new Olympic all-around champion and congratulated her on a convincing victory.

When Shawn later accepted her silver medal, she received sizable cheers from the audience. The beloved gymnast hadn't won the color medal she desired, but gymnastics fans everywhere still adored her.

Later when asked about her second place finish, Shawn showed great pride with her placement.

Nastia and Shawn go 1,2 in the Olympic all-around.
(Photo by Getty Images)

"I'm so proud to be wearing the silver medal," she remarked. "I was happy and proud throughout the whole thing. It's just been a long road and I'm really happy that I'm here."

Some of Shawn's Many Fans
(Photo by Ricardo Bufolin)

Shawn's parents were bursting with pride at their daughter's momentous accomplishment. At the end of the evening, Teri and Doug looked just as emotional as Shawn.

"It was one of the most awesome meets I've ever seen her compete in," Shawn's father exclaimed. "We were very proud of her."

When Chow expressed admiration for his star pupil, he echoed the thoughts of so many sports fans.

"She is a truly strong individual. Not only a wonderful, top-notch gymnast, but she's a great individual as well," he praised. "I'm so proud of what she has done. I cannot say enough good things about this kid."

"Beam has always been one of my stronger events. I've always loved the beam. I've loved taking the risks of all the hard skills that I do."

Event Finals

Beijing 2008

Two opportunities remained for Shawn to win an Olympic gold medal. Champions would be crowned in four apparatuses. She qualified for two events: floor and balance beam.

The first participant on the floor, Shawn dressed in a striking royal blue costume. She delivered another marvelous performance. The affable teen then smiled brightly after receiving her score of 15.5.

Afterwards, Shawn and Chow watched as the other competitors tried to top her score. Nastia delivered another lyrical performance on floor but came up just short with a 15.425. Only Romania's Sandra Izbasa managed to outscore the early leader. When the floor final ended, Shawn had captured a third straight silver medal.

Though Shawn felt grateful to medal, she couldn't help wishing for a gold souvenir to take home. Would it ever happen?

On the day of balance beam finals, Shawn felt physically and emotionally fatigued. She suffered from an upset stomach

Shawn Johnson - Olympic Champion.
(Photo by Getty Images)

and a headache. During warm-up on her best apparatus, she fell seven times.

Chow needed to wake up his student. He pulled her aside for an invigorating big pep talk. Suddenly, Shawn snapped to attention. She was at the Olympics for goodness sake! No way would she leave Beijing without giving her absolute best in her final performance.

When it came time to compete, Shawn unleashed a splendid beam program. When she landed her difficult dismount, she smiled in jubilation. The judges rewarded her with a score of 16.225. Now she would wait to see if anyone could beat it.

Gymnast after gymnast, including Nastia, strived to outdo Shawn. No one could reach the high standard she set.

When the beam competition ended, Shawn snared the gold medal. She was an Olympic champion! An emotional Shawn hugged Chow and waved to her fans in the stands. Even her competitors seemed happy for her.

"I was pulling for her," Nastia, who finished second, remarked. "She finally got that gold. She deserved it 100%."

Shawn placed her hand over her heart and watched her country's flag raised as the *Star Spangled Banner* played throughout the arena. Her gold medal beamed nearly as bright as her contagious smile.

"It's been the best Olympic experience ever," Shawn declared after the medal ceremony. "The emotions are indescribable."

She paused for a moment before adding, "It was the perfect ending."

"I don't feel like a star; I never have."

Post-Olympics

Shawn Johnson almost didn't make it home to the United States. During her plane's boarding process, the pilot learned that she was on board. He stood up quickly in a rush to meet her and hit his head, requiring multiple stitches. The passengers then waited for some time as the airline searched for a replacement pilot!

When Shawn landed in America, she went straight to a taping of *Late Show with David Letterman*. Suffering from acute jet lag, Shawn walked out onto the stage, shook hands with the famous talk show host and quipped, "I'm really thankful for the makeup and hair artists."

Everyone wanted to interview the new Olympic champion. Shawn jetted everywhere to fulfill interview requests. She danced with Ellen and even chatted with Oprah.

When she finally returned home to West Des Moines, her hometown threw her a massive celebration. 7,000 Iowans filed into the Wells Fargo Arena. Organizers hadn't expected such a massive turnout, and they scrambled to provide additional seating.

"Why would you come out here for me?" the modest teenager asked the crowd. "It doesn't make sense, but it's amazing."

Just days later, Shawn flew to Denver, Colorado, and led the pledge of allegiance before 75,000 people at the 2008 Democratic National Convention. Wearing a Team USA blouse and a simple black skirt, she remained on stage while Academy Award winner Jennifer Hudson sang the national anthem. She even met former Vice President Al Gore!

Shawn's Cheerios Box

On October 7, 2008, Shawn landed in Washington D.C. for an important date - with the President of the United States. Shawn and other American Olympians were honored for representing the United States at the Beijing Olympics. She stood behind First Lady Laura Bush while President George W. Bush delivered a speech on the South Lawn of the White House.

Shawn and Regis Philbin
(Photo by ABC TV)

Shawn acts on *The Secret Life of the American Teenager.*
(Photo by ABCFamily)

The honors and high-profile appearances kept piling up for Shawn. The Iowa Hall of Pride in Des Moines unveiled a bronze sculpture of her on a balance beam for all visitors to see. She also appeared opposite Regis Philbin on the celebrity edition of *Who Wants to Be a Millionaire?*, winning 50,000 dollars for Blank Children's Hospital. Shawn even served as a judge for the Miss America pageant!

Shawn's Video Game

Shawn then debuted a gymnastics clothing line. She teamed with GK Elite to present the Shawn Johnson Signature Leotard and Shorts Collection. The colorful clothes featured Shawn's signature, as well as peace and heart graphics.

"I hope everyone finds my collection to be fun and fashionable," she remarked.

Shawn also became immortalized in a video game! The teenager was floored when Nintendo Wii approached her about branding a gymnastics game in her name. *Shawn Johnson Gymnastics* allowed gamers the chance to create various routines while competing in world gymnastics competitions!

The in-demand teenager even dabbled with an acting career when she filmed two episodes of the popular *ABC Family* series *The Secret Life of the American Teenager*. A big fan of the show, Shawn felt so excited when she arrived on the set and filmed a scene with one of its stars, Daren Kagasoff.

Despite all her amazing opportunities, gymnastics still ruled Shawn's heart. That's why she adored headlining the 2008 *Tour of Gymnastics Superstars*. The family oriented show traveled the country and featured top gymnasts performing various routines set to popular music. Shawn and Nastia opened every show together, and the crowd always showered them with a standing ovation.

2008 Gymnastics Tour

Shawn performed several solo routines in the show. Sporting a pink tank top and a black skirt, she displayed her playful side and played air guitar in a spunky floor exercise to Miley Cyrus' *Rockstar*. She also showed a more mature side with a sophisticated program to Rihanna's *Don't Stop the Music.*

Shawn - Avid Reader

Of course, gymnastics lovers clamored to watch Shawn excel on her signature apparatus, the balance beam. Each night she showed off an exquisite routine set to Chris Brown's "Dreamer," an inspirational song written specifically for U.S. Olympians.

Shawn presents at the Teen Choice Awards.
(Photo by FOX TV)

After the action-packed show, Shawn's fans flocked to souvenir stands. Among a slew of flashy memorabilia, gymnastics buffs could purchase sweatshirts, backpacks and t-shirts bearing Shawn's name and image. Every night, satisfied little girls left arenas clutching Shawn Johnson merchandise!

The tour also afforded the down-to-earth teenager time to reconnect with her gymnast friends. Chellsie Memmel, Bridget Sloan, Samantha Peszek and Shayla Worley also performed on the tour. They were joined by gymnastics legends Shannon Miller and Paul Hamm! The close-knit group loved traveling on a tour bus where they played games, like Nintendo Wii's *Guitar Hero*.

Wherever Shawn traveled, though, people asked the same question. Would she return to competition someday? Might she attempt a bid at the 2012 London Olympics?

"I'd give anything to feel that again," Shawn responded. "If I can, I'll be there."

Shawn as a WallStar
(Photo by WallStars.TV)

"I don't think I can be perfect because I'm not a professional ballroom dancer, but I'm just going to do my best."

Dancing with the Stars

In early 2009, Shawn received exciting news. *ABC* asked her to participate in season eight of *Dancing with the Stars*, a popular reality show where celebrities compete against each other alongside professional dance partners. Shawn couldn't believe she would appear on her favorite show!

Shawn's wish also came true when the producers partnered her with Mark Ballas, a seasoned ballroom dancer. Mark won the reality show competition one year earlier with his partner, Olympic gold medal figure skater, Kristi Yamaguchi. Although the youngest competitor in the history of the show, Shawn already knew she could rely on Mark as a partner!

Shawn's fellow contestants this season included Grammy Award-winning rapper Lil' Kim, Apple Co-Founder Steve Wozniak and French actor Gilles Marini.

Some people assumed Shawn had the competitive edge due to her gymnastics background. Once Shawn began attending rehearsal however, she realized nothing could be further from the truth. While gymnastics encouraged rigid precision, dance required elegant and smooth movements.

In their first week, Shawn and Mark performed a waltz. In rehearsal, Shawn found it difficult to pull off such a romantic dance. In fact, she had to stop herself from giggling non-stop! A nervous Shawn began to wonder if she was ready for such a competition. On the first episode, things got off to a rocky start. During the opening, Shawn tripped while walking down a flight of stairs. Thankfully, Mark caught Shawn before

Shawn competes on *Dancing with the Stars*.
(Photo by ABC TV)

she fell. Earlier in the week, Mark convinced Shawn she could dance in three-inch heels. The pint-sized gymnast wasn't used to wearing heels after competing barefoot for so many years!

That evening, an anxious Shawn took the stage to perform her first dance on live television. She desperately wanted to perform well and make her partner proud. She donned a long, flowing sequined yellow dress, satin gloves and sparkly jewelry – a far cry from her usual costume of just a one-piece leotard!

As the first few notes of Dana Glover's "It is You (I Have Loved)" played, Shawn and Mark began twirling and spinning around the stage with their hands locked. As Shawn showcased some tricks like high kicks and low dips, her uncertainty seemed to melt away. The duo nailed their first routine.

Once they finished their dance, the pair listened to the critiques of the three-judge panel. Judge Carrie Ann Inaba praised Shawn for her excellent footwork and ability to move people through dance, despite her young age. Judge Bruno Tonioli agreed and admitted shock over Shawn's seemingly effortless elegance and refinement, while judge Len Goodman deemed the performance as simply fantastic.

In terms of scoring, the show combined the judges' scores with the call-in votes from the audience at home. Each week, the couple with the lowest point total went home. Their graceful routine helped keep Shawn and Mark from getting cut!

As the weeks progressed, Shawn developed a strong, almost-brotherly bond with her partner.

"She's great," agreed Mark. "We have a lot of fun in the studio and we laugh a lot. At the same time, we buckle down and work really hard."

Mark continually looked after Shawn both on and off-camera. For instance, with the show filming in Los Angeles, Shawn missed out on her senior prom. As a result, one day, Mark brought the prom to her! He filled the rehearsal space with balloons and flowers. Mark even showed up dressed in a tuxedo and provided Shawn with a glitzy gold dress so they could dance together just like prom!

Of course, the two joked around a lot, too. For instance, Mark habitually teased Shawn about her short attention span. Sometimes he would be explaining a move to the teenager when her mind would start wandering, and he'd have to beg her to refocus! Meanwhile, Shawn liked to kid Mark about his overuse of certain words. In particular, she claimed he said "epic" too much and enjoyed teasing him about it!

Over the course of the next few weeks, the close-knit duo performed a variety of dances, including a salsa, foxtrot, Viennese waltz and rumba. The judges and audience continued to marvel at Shawn's confidence and polished dance skills.

A ton of supporters around the country rooted for Shawn. Back home, her friends hosted viewing parties and cheered for their dear friend. Devoted fans of the duo combined Shawn and Mark's first names, giving them the nickname, Team Shark. Each week, her proud parents sat in the studio audience rooting for their little girl. Cameras caught them grinning wildly, week after week, as Shawn continued to shine.

Shawn and Partner Mark Ballas
(Photo by ABC TV)

Unfortunately, Shawn and her family dealt with some serious problems during this time as well. One of Shawn's older male fans became obsessed with the young gymnast. At one point, the aggressive man decided he wanted to meet Shawn and drove halfway across the country to find her. He even tried to crash the *Dancing with the Stars* set in the hopes of meeting her.

Shawn's understandably nervous parents moved quickly to protect their daughter. They were granted a restraining order against the man, which legally required him to stay far away from Shawn. As an added precaution, the *Dancing with the Stars'* studio provided extra security for the Olympian.

Thankfully Shawn blocked out the distractions and continued enjoying her time on the show. She also learned to let loose as the competition went on, particularly during the week when they performed a Lindy Hop. To prepare for the truly athletic dance filled with tumbling tricks, Mark and Shawn trained at a gym that week. While Shawn felt right at home in the gym, Mark worked outside of his comfort zone for once!

Mark simply marveled as he watched the gold medal gymnast flipping through the gym.

"When you have a partner who's the best in the world at what they do, getting to see it up close and personal, it's just out of this world," Mark gushed.

During week seven, Shawn faced even more challenges, including a hectic schedule filled with prior commitments. As a result, Mark flew to Iowa to meet Shawn for rehearsals. During their limited practice time together, the pair scrambled to learn a complex cha-cha-cha routine to Michael Jackson's

Glamorous Shawn dances Before millions.
(Photo by ABC TV)

Shawn and Mark Ballas
(Photo by ABC TV)

"P.Y.T. (Pretty Young Thing)." The teenager felt completely overwhelmed.

Amazingly, Shawn still rose to the challenge. The evening of the performance, the gymnast looked like a seasoned dancer, busting out some fast and funky moves. As a result, Bruno rewarded the pair with their first perfect 10 score in the competition!

Ever the competitor, Shawn made it her goal to earn even more 10's throughout the rest of the competition! The following week, rewarded for their hard work and effortless dancing, the pair received a 10 from Carrie Ann for their samba to Kool and the Gang's "Get Down On It." Yet Shawn still craved more, and the next week, while performing a Paso Doble, they earned two perfect 10's from both Carrie Ann and Bruno!

Week 10 served as the most important set of performances to date as it determined whether or not Shawn and Mark qualified for the finals. Their dance for the week, a slow and passionate Argentine tango, required a mixture of sophistication and complex moves. Things did not look promising in rehearsal however when the pair struggled with mistimed lifts and spins.

The night of the actual competition, the anxiety-ridden twosome took to the floor. As soon as the music began, Mark and Shawn began to move as one. In a routine filled with raw emotion and intensity, Shawn and Mark earned a perfect 30, with all three judges delivering 10's! The judges' scores, combined with the viewers' votes, secured the pair a spot in the finals!

Reality star Melissa Rycroft and partner Tony Dovolani, as well as Gilles and his dance partner, Cheryl Burke, also made the finals.

The first night of the two-part finale, all three couples battled serious nerves. Adding to the mounting tension, the dancers performed three different routines over the course of two nights.

The first performance of the evening, a group Paso Doble number to Pink's "So What," highlighted each of the three pairs with a solo dance section. Although Shawn and Mark received a 10, all of the couples looked fantastic. In fact, following the first round, Team Shark sat in third place by the slimmest of margins.

Next up, Shawn and Mark performed a freestyle dance to "Do Your Thing" by Basement Jaxx. Dressed in jump suits and white masks, the jive-like piece included high-energy flips, fast-paced steps and perfectly synchronized tumbles. The judges raved about the performance, causing a joyous Shawn to leap towards the judges' table, planting a kiss on each of their cheeks. Not surprisingly, the couple received a perfect score of 30 for the performance!

The following evening, more than 20 million viewers tuned in to watch the three-way showdown live. The jam-packed show included performances by Lady Gaga, as well as dances by contestants from throughout the season.

Eventually, the competition portion resumed, starting with Shawn and Mark's final performance. The couple opted to repeat Shawn's breakthrough performance to "P.Y.T. (Pretty Young Thing)." Dressed in a black and cream sequined dress, Shawn delivered an even stronger performance than her original. She positively beamed throughout the dance, displaying a confident and gleeful attitude.

The judges marveled at Shawn's marked improvement over the course of just a few weeks. Carrie Ann claimed that everyone clearly underestimated her ability. As the final cherry on top, the routine also received a perfect 30!

Receiving seven perfect 10's over the course of two evenings, Shawn and Mark appeared on track to easily win the title. Yet, in a remarkable turn of events, Gilles and Cheryl received identical marks! Ultimately, the voting audience at home would break the tie in this nail-biting competition!

Once all the contestants finished performing, the lights dimmed. Hosts Tom Bergeron and Samantha Harris began announcing the results. Melissa and Tony were the first couple eliminated from the show. The competition came down to Shawn and Mark versus Gilles and Cheryl!

As they hugged each other tightly, Mark and Shawn held their breath. Tom announced the vote margin between the two couples came in at less than 1%, making it the show's closest finale ever.

An overwhelming sense of anxiety and excitement filled the studio.

Tom finally broke the silence.

"After 11 hard-fought weeks of competition, the winners and new champions of *Dancing with the Stars* are: Shawn and Mark!"

Upon hearing the news, Shawn let out a loud scream before clasping her hand firmly over her mouth in utter shock.

The champion gymnast and dancer leapt into Mark's arms as he spun her around the dance floor. With confetti falling from the ceiling, all of the competitors rushed the stage, joining Mark and Shawn in their celebration. While Mark fell to the floor in amazement, country singer and former contestant Chuck Wicks hoisted Shawn on his shoulders for a victory lap!

Once the cameras turned off, a horde of reporters descended upon the crowned champions.

When asked her thoughts on the win, Shawn proclaimed, "I'm feeling like the happiest girl in the world. I worked so hard for this, come so far and grown as a person. This has changed my life. I owe everything to Mark."

Her partner did not seem the least bit surprised by Shawn's talent as a dancer.

"I believed in Shawn from day one and was just honored to be her partner," he announced.

When asked to compare the win to her other achievements, Shawn paused for a beat.

"It feels like another gold medal," Shawn beamed, while clutching her mirror ball trophy.

The Happy Winners
(Photo by ABC TV)

"It takes a lot of confidence to be in the public eye."

No End in Sight

On April 15 2009, Shawn Johnson arrived in New York as a nominee for sports' most esteemed award: The James E. Sullivan Award. Presented by the American Amateur Athletic Union (AAU), the award is presented annually to "the outstanding amateur athlete in the United States," with special attention to leadership, character, sportsmanship and the ideals of amateurism. The Sullivan Award, as it's often called, has been labeled the Oscar® of sports awards. Past recipients include Mark Spitz, Michael Phelps, Florence Griffith-Joyner, Janet Evans, Dan Jansen, Michelle Kwan and Peyton Manning.

In Shawn's particular year, she faced a strong lineup. Finalists included Nastia Liukin, the U.S. Olympic men's 400-meter freestyle relay swim team; volleyball player Cynthia Barboza of Stanford; and North Carolina basketball player Tyler Hansbrough.

Not expecting to win, Shawn showed up to the ceremony just honored to be included in an exceptional list of nominees. Imagine her shock then when she was announced as the winner! The tiny teenager looked stunned as she made her way to the stage to deliver a speech.

"Thank you. It's an honor to be recognized with this award," she stated. "Any athlete that puts that much hard work into it deserves to be recognized. This has been the craziest year of my life, and I've loved every second of it. I couldn't have gotten here without my parents and coaches. I'm so happy and honored to represent the sport of gymnastics."

"This is an incredible honor for Shawn," Steve Penny, President of USA Gymnastics, remarked. "It recognizes her outstanding gymnastics accomplishments, as well as her character both on and off the field of play."

With her celebrity rising, Shawn enjoyed the perks of being a celebrity. Among the film premieres she attended: *Transformers 2, Terminator Salvation, Hannah Montana: The Movie, Star Trek, Jonas Brothers: The 3D Concert Experience* and *Twilight Saga: Eclipse.* Shawn, and her *Dancing with the Stars* partner, Mark Ballas, even presented at the Country Music Awards.

Shawn and her mom play Nintendo.
(Photo by Nintendo)

Of course, Shawn still received awards, too. In July of 2009, she arrived at the ESPYs, ESPN's yearly sports award show, in a flowing pink dress. Moments later, she appeared on stage to accept the trophy for Best U.S. Female Olympian. A popular fixture at the Teen Choice Awards, Shawn won Choice Female Athlete on three occasions. In a 2009 national poll, conducted by E-Poll Market Research, America named her the most-liked sports figure!

Many young girls looked up to Shawn, and she took her role model status very seriously. The Olympic champion accepted public speaking engagements all across the country and spoke to young people about healthy living. In particular, she stressed the importance of education, physical fitness and good eating habits.

Though Shawn no longer trained as rigorously as she once did, she still occasionally visited Chow's Gymnastics to maintain certain gymnastics skills. In fall of 2009, she even

Shawn meets a young fan.
(Photo by Jerry Logsdon)

challenged herself to run a 1/2 marathon at the Des Moines Marathon. She finished the event in two hours, thirteen minutes and twenty-one seconds.

In December of 2010, Shawn and her parents flew to Colorado for a much-deserved family vacation. While skiing on a mountain slope, she took a nasty spill and began experiencing pain in her right knee. A doctor pronounced Shawn with a tear in one of her knee's major ligaments. A surgeon performed surgery and forbid the gymnast from doing gymnastics for several months.

Hours after her surgery, a despondent Shawn lay in her hospital bed. As she looked at her wrapped knee, one thought dominated her mind: What if she could never compete again?

Suddenly, a pang of dread ran through her body. The idea of leaving competitive gymnastics for good left her crushed and frantic. She quickly realized that she was not ready to retire from competition.

Over the next few days, Shawn's hospital room bustled with visitors, flowers and get-well cards. Though it all, she felt distracted by two nagging words:

London 2012.

"I'm completely different than 2008. I'm three or four years older and going into this as the new Shawn."

The Comeback

In spring of 2010, Shawn appeared at Hy-Vee's Exercise Your Character event in Des Moines, Iowa. 8,000 children listened ardently to their hometown hero as she stressed the importance of sportsmanship and strong character.

As Shawn left the stage after the motivational talk, a Hy-Vee representative asked the crowd if they wanted the gymnast to return for a run at the 2012 London Olympics. As they roared with delight, the teenage idol stopped short in her tracks, returned to the stage and grabbed a microphone.

"About London," she began, flashing her trademark smile. "I don't know if you know, but I am going to give it a shot. I'm going to go for it."

News of Shawn's announcement spread quickly throughout the sports world. Newspapers carried headlines of her intended comeback. Many expressed delight at the notion of Shawn returning to competition.

"I was going to do a formal press conference and announce it that way, in front of cameras," she told the *Des Moines Register*. "But I got caught up in the moment. And what better way to do it than to inspire 8,000 kids?"

After Shawn fully recovered from her knee injury, she returned to her home training center. The Iowa native would

Shawn thought long & hard about making a comeback.
(Photo by Ricardo Bufolin)

164

again seek a trip to the Olympics under Coach Chow. She wouldn't have it any other way.

Resuming heavy training proved a challenging feat for Shawn. Some days she even questioned her decision. Then she would regain a difficult skill, and an adrenalin rush invigorated her and reminded her why she loved gymnastics. After so many years, she still thrived on the thrill of working hard and achieving a tough goal.

On July 23, 2011, Shawn returned to competition when she entered the 2011 CoverGirl Classic in Chicago, Illinois. Because she opted to gradually ease back into gymnastics, Shawn chose to compete only on bars and balance beam. Her surgically repaired knee needed more time to adapt to floor exercise and vault.

Prior to leaving Des Moines for the Windy City, Shawn took to her official Twitter account to release some tension.

"On my way to Chicago!" she tweeted: "#butterflies #heartattack #anxiety hah!"

Hours before the competition, Shawn popped back online to write: "Trying to nap before tonight HAH! Not possible... Adrenaline already going... I think I'm going to be sick ;)."

When the arena announcer called Shawn's name, a massive roar emanated from the crowd. Competitive gymnastics had missed their smiling golden girl. Although Shawn performed a shaky balance beam program, she felt thrilled to finally get back into competition. She then exhibited a strong bars routine with only a stumble on her dismount.

Shawn at the 2011 Pan Am Games
(Photo by Ricardo Bufolin)

Shawn and Bridgette Caquatto
(Photo by Ricardo Bufolin)

"The skills are there. She just might not have enough time under her belt," remarked an *NBC* announcer.

Thankfully, Shawn had a short trip home. Back in Des Moines, she began training hard for the U.S. Championships that were only a month away. Shawn desperately wanted to improve upon her performances from CoverGirl Classic.

In late August, the popular gymnast arrived in Minnesota for the 2011 Visa Championships. The last time Shawn competed in St. Paul, she was a junior competitor trying to make her mark in the gymnastics world. Now she stood out as the seasoned veteran making a much-publicized return to her sport.

Shawn elected to compete in only three events at nationals: balance beam, uneven bars and vault. As she hoped, the strong competitor improved greatly on her performances from CoverGirl Classic.

Shawn Back on the Beam
(Photo by Ricardo Bufolin)

Shawn and Chow - Together Again
(Photo by Ricardo Bufolin)

"I'm by no means back to where I want to be, but I've made a huge improvement," she remarked with a huge smile.

At the end of the competition, USA Gymnastics named Shawn to the national team! For the first time in nearly three years, she would be eligible to represent the United States in international competition.

A few weeks later, Shawn was back training at the Karolyi Camp and under serious consideration for the world team. She felt shocked beyond belief. All along, she set a goal of competing at the 2012 Olympics and never dreamed she would contend for any international competitions this season.

As it turned out, Marta named Shawn as a non-traveling alternate for the 2011 World Championship team. Plus, she selected the gymnast to lead the team at that fall's Pan Am Games.

In October that year, Shawn landed in Guadalajara, Mexico, for her first international competition since the

The Happy Medal Winners
(Photo by Ricardo Bufolin)

Beijing Olympics. She felt honored to once again represent her country on a major stage.

By the end of the 2011 Pan Am Games, Shawn wore familiar hardware. A gold medal dangled from her neck. She and her teammates took first place in the team competition. A few days later, she added a silver medal to her collection with a strong uneven bars routine.

Shawn Johnson was back and loved gymnastics even more than ever. As she looked toward the future, the 2012 London Olympics became more and more clear to her. Whatever hap-

Shawn vaults to victory.
(Photo by Ricardo Bufolin)

Shawn competes in team finals at the Pan Am Games.
(Photo by Ricardo Bufolin)

pened, though, she would hold no regrets. How can one ever regret pursuing something that brought so much joy?

When discussing her comeback, Shawn perfectly summed up why she still loved competing in gymnastics after so many years.

"Getting to wear the red, white and blue again, it brings me chills," she gushed. "It's such an honor. It's exciting. I love every second of it. I love being back, and it's only motivating me more and more. I'm finally back, and I love it."

Shawn returns and wins gold.
(Photo by Ricardo Bufolin)

Shawn - Forever A Champion
(Photo by Ricardo Bufolin)

Essential Shawn Johnson Links

Shawn's Official Page
www.ShawnJohnson.net

Shawn's Twitter
www.Twitter.com/ShawnJohnson

Shawn Fan Page
www.Shawn-Johnson.us

USA Gymnastics
www.USAGym.org

WallStars
www.WallStars.tv

Author Page
www.ChristineDzidrums.com

GymnStars Books
www.GymnStars.com

Ricardo Bufolin's Photography
www.flickr.com/photos/ricardobufolin/

Tomas Tyrpekl Photography
www.flickr.com/photos/tmsworkshop/

GymBox
www.gymbox.net/

Build Your SkateStars™ Collection Today!

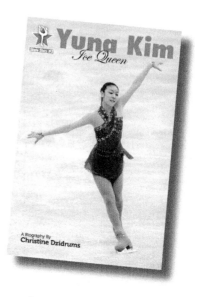

At the 2010 Vancouver Olympics, tragic circumstances thrust **Joannie Rochette** into the international spotlight when her beloved mother died two days before the ladies short program. The world held their breath for the bereaved figure skater when she opted to compete in her mom's memory. Joannie then captured hearts everywhere when she courageously skated two moving programs to win the Olympic bronze medal. *Joannie Rochette: Canadian Ice Princess* reveals answers to ice skating enthusiasts' most asked questions.

Meet figure skating's biggest star: **Yuna Kim**. The Korean trailblazer produced two legendary performances at the 2010 Vancouver Olympic Games to win the gold medal in convincing fashion. *Yuna Kim: Ice Queen*, the second book in the **Skate Stars** series, uncovers the compelling story of how the beloved figure skater overcame poor training conditions, various injuries and numerous other obstacles to become world and Olympic champion.

About the Authors

Christine Dzidrums holds a bachelor's degree in Theater Arts from California State University, Fullerton. She previously co-wrote *Joannie Rochette: Canadian Ice Princess* and *Yuna Kim: Ice Queen* . Her first novel, *Cutters Don't Cry*, won a 2010 Moonbeam Children's Book Award in the Young Adult Fiction category. Christine also authored the picture book, *Princess Dessabelle Makes a Friend*. She recently competed her second novel, *Kaylee: The 'What If?' Game*.

Leah Rendon graduated with a Bachelor of Arts degree from the University of California, Los Angeles. She co-authored the children's sports' biography, *Joannie Rochette: Canadian Ice Princess*. Throughout her writing career she has covered major skating events, including the Winter Olympic Games, the Grand Prix Series and the World Figure Skating Championships. She has also interviewed many top athletes, including Olympic champions Katarina Witt, Brian Boitano and Oksana Baiul.

Also From

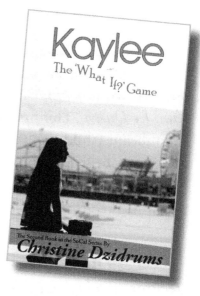

2010 Moonbeam Children's Book Award Winner! In a series of raw journal entries written to her absentee father, a teenager chronicles her penchant for self-harm, a serious struggle with depression and an inability to vocally express her feelings.

"I play the 'What If?'" game all the time. It's a cruel, wicked game."

Meet free spirit Kaylee Matthews, the most popular girl in school. But when the teenager suffers a devastating loss, her sunny personality turns dark as she struggles with debilitating panic attacks and unresolved anger. Can Kaylee repair her broken spirit, or will she forever remain a changed person?

Meet Princess Dessabelle, a spoiled, lonely princess with a quick temper. When she orders a kind classmate to be her friend, she learns the true meaning of friendship.